100
AFTERNOON
SWEETS

100

AFTER

SWEE

with Snacking Cakes, Brownies,
Blondies, and More

SARAH KIEFFER

NOON

TS

CHRONICLE BOOKS
SAN FRANCISCO

Library of Congress Cataloging-in-Publication Data available.

ISBN 978-1-7972-1618-8

Manufactured in China.

Food styling by Sarah Kieffer.
Design by Lizzie Vaughan.
Typesetting by Taylor Roy.

10 9 8 7 6 5 4 3 2 1

Chronicle books and gifts are available at special quantity discounts to corporations, professional associations, literacy programs, and other organizations. For details and discount information, please contact our premiums department at corporatesales@chroniclebooks.com or at 1-800-759-0190.

Chronicle Books LLC
680 Second Street
San Francisco, California 94107
www.chroniclebooks.com

DEDICATION

TO LARRY AND COLLEEN—

Every successful attempt in my kitchen and every recipe I have written have their roots in the Blue Heron Coffeehouse. You taught me so much about baking, cooking, and running a business. But the ways you see and care for people have made the biggest impact on my life. Thank you for taking a chance on me all those years ago. Also, I promise I will never again spill grape juice concentrate all over my spare tire and then make you clean out my trunk and change my flat. I love you both.

Contents

Introduction 11

1

ONE-BOWL BAKES

2

BROWNIES, BLONDIES, AND BARS

1) My Perfect Afternoon Snacking Cake 30

2) Confetti Cake with Berry Buttercream 32

3) Classic Crumb Cake 34

4) Straight-Up Yellow Snacking Cake 37

5) Raspberry Poppy Seed Cake 38

6) Cranberry Caramel Upside-Down Cake 40

7) Blueberry Muffin Cake 42

8) Banana Bread Bars 45

9) Maple Orange Carrot Cake 46

10) Honey Sesame Cake 49

11) Jam-Filled Doughnut Cake 50

12) Classic Birthday Cake 52

13) Coconut Chocolate Chip Cake 54

14) Chocolate Red Wine Cake 56

15) Double Chocolate Cake 58

16) Brownies 2.0 64

17) Milk Chocolate Swirl Brownies 67

18) White Chocolate, Dark Chocolate Brownies 69

19) Banana Bread Brownies 72

20) Brown Butter Banana Blondies 74

21) Bourbon Blondies 76

22) Scotcharoo Blondies 78

23) Toasted Sesame Blondies 81

24) Sugar Cookie Bars 82

25) Raisin Rum Bars 84

26) Creamy Raspberry Bars 86

27) Lemon Cake Squares 88

28) Chocolate Rye Cookie Bars 90

29) Chocolate Meringue Bars 92

30) Pecan Espresso Bars 94

31) Chocolate Chip Bars 97

32) Oatmeal Fudge Bars 98

3

PIE BAKES

33) Millionaire Pie 105

34) Chocolate Peanut Butter Pie 107

35) Chocolate Irish Cream Mousse Pie 110

36) Smoky Butterscotch Cream Pie 112

37) Lemon White Chocolate Pie 114

38) Lemon Meringue Pie 116

39) Apple Cider Pie 118

40) Mixed Berry Cheesecake Slab Pie 121

41) Passion Fruit S'mores Pie 123

42) Roasted Strawberry Cream Pie 125

43) Pumpkin Streusel Pie 127

44) Rhubarb and Cream Hand Pies 129

45) Banana Cream Pie 132

4

NO BAKES

46) Mint Chocolate Ice Cream Bars 138

47) Red Velvet Ice Cream Cake 140

48) Pumpkin Caramel Ice Cream Cake 143

49) Strawberry Balsamic Shortcake Ice Cream Bars 145

50) Neapolitan Ice Cream Bars 148

51) Passion Fruit Slice 151

52) Kitchen Sink Crispy Treats 153

53) Chocolate Cheesecake 154

54) Peanut Butter Chocolate Bars 156

55) S'mores Bars 159

56) Chocolate Éclair Cake 161

57) White Chocolate Raspberry Squares 164

5

FOR A CROWD

58) Coffee Blondies 171

59) Rocky Road Brownies 172

60) Raspberry Almond Coffee
Cake Squares 174

61) Raspberry Mascarpone
Cheesecake Tart 176

62) Blueberry Crumble Bars 178

63) Pumpkin Bars 180

64) Cherry Pie Bars 182

65) Strawberry Shortcake Cake 185

66) Lemon Streusel Squares 188

67) Pretzel Shortbread Fingers 190

68) Caramel Rhubarb Shortbread Bars 192

69) Peanut Butter and Jelly Cake 194

70) Minnesota Sheet Cake 196

6

WEEKEND PROJECTS

71) Orange-Cinnamon Swirl Cake 202

72) Maple Bourbon Sticky Bun Cake 204

73) Hazelnut Frangipane Cake 207

74) Sunken Chocolate Cake 210

75) Fig Scones 212

76) Brownie Cheesecake Bars 215

77) Chocolate Chip Buttermilk Cake 218

78) Tiramisu Cake 221

79) White Chocolate Cheesecake 224

80) Picnic Cakes 227

81) Giant Pop Tart 230

82) Pavlova 233

83) Apricot Almond Croissant 234

84) Gluten-Free Cake 236

7

BEGINNINGS AND ENDS

85) Swiss Meringue Buttercream 242

86) American Buttercream 245

87) Ermine Buttercream 246

88) Ultra Buttercream 249

89) Cream Cheese Buttercream 250

90) Peanut Butter Buttercream 253

91) Bittersweet Chocolate Buttercream 254

92) Fudge Buttercream 256

93) Ganache 257

94) Meringue 258

95) Pie Dough 261

96) Pat-in-the-Pan Pie Dough 262

97) Crème Fraîche Dough 263

98) Cheater Croissant Dough 264

99) Rough Puff Pastry 268

100) Chocolate Wafer Cookies 270

8

EXTRAS

Caramel 276

Brown Butter 276

Crème Fraîche 278

Whipped Cream 278

Pastry Cream 279

Almond Cream 281

Lemon Curd 282

No-Churn Ice Cream 283

Candied Nuts 284

Streusel 287

Pecan Streusel 287

Candied Cacao Nibs 288

Chocolate Magic Shell 288

Music to Bake To 293

Conversions 294

Bibliography 295

Resources 296

Acknowledgments 297

Index 300

Introduction

When I started baking more than twenty-five years ago, I never could have imagined that all those kitchen counters I worked from would lead me here, writing the introduction to my fifth cookbook. Writing a book was my dream since my short-story phase in middle school, and while at the time I had envisioned writing more of a Nancy Drew mystery meets *Beverly Hills, 90210* book series, I am still very happy to have found my way to writing cookbooks.

My baking adventures started in ninth grade, slowly fizzled out in high school, then reignited in college at the Blue Heron Coffeehouse, where Larry and Colleen Wolner gave me a chance in their kitchen as their first employee. After college, I put baking professionally on hold and found jobs as both a bookseller and barista simultaneously. But the kitchen gods called to me, and the door to baking opened unexpectedly again. This time I was the sole baker in a newly opened coffeehouse on the University of Minnesota campus, in charge of developing the recipes as well as everything else involved in the tiny, sweltering kitchen: baking, washing dishes, prepping, cleaning, and more baking. I learned a lot on my own,

figuring it out while failing forward. Several years later, my husband and I decided to expand our family, and, weighing the cost and stress of child care, I decided to take a break from baking and moved on to full-time parenting. The years I spent at home with my two little ones were beautiful, challenging, and fulfilling, but the butter and eggs and sugar frequently whispered to me. After my son was born, I started a simple website, the *Vanilla Bean Blog*, as an outlet for my writing and baking habits that were overtaking our kitchen counters. Over the years, my site slowly grew its viewership, and out of the work I put in there, I found myself submitting a proposal to a publisher and then writing my first cookbook. It has been almost ten years since I started that first book, and I have put my ten thousand hours in to master some skills, although almost every day in the kitchen shows there is still, always, much more to learn.

People ask me the most important things to know about baking, often looking for tips, tricks, and shortcuts. I find that many people are intimidated by baking. Maybe it's the science and math involved or the small margin for error that can feel overwhelming to some. So I tell them several things to remember as they attempt recipes, the first being this: When baking in my early twenties, I didn't care about or understand the importance of weighing flour or following a recipe exactly as written—baking was just fun! I made a lot of mistakes, but, more importantly, I found an interest that challenged me and gave me purpose as I experimented in my own way.

The second thing I tell people: In each book I've written, I respect the presence of the "kitchen gods"—a belief that Larry Wolner instilled in me years ago while working at the Blue Heron. During my years there, I spent a lot of time making banana bread. It was one of my daily tasks, and after hundreds of hours of mixing and mashing, I could have made the bread in my sleep. However, one Friday afternoon, after making it had become more routine than pleasure, I baked four loaves that sunk in the middle and tasted terrible. Larry walked over to my prep table to take a peek at the wasted loaves, and I'll never forget his words: "The kitchen gods are always watching," he said. "You may think you have a recipe down, but

the minute you feel you own a recipe or lack humbleness, the gods will remind you of your place in things." His sincerity in the moment etched those sentences in my mind, and I recall them often.

My imagination often runs wild, so picturing the gods of the kitchen hovering over me is not a far-fetched notion. But, as with many myths, their lessons are all about life here on the terra firma, even in our kitchens. I've found that when I assume what I make will turn out perfectly, I am often unconsciously careless and make a mistake. It's not that being confident in my skills is wrong, but repeatedly not taking a moment to acknowledge the recipe with its instructions and ingredients and notes and history can make for a less-than-successful outcome.

Which brings me to the third thing I tell people: Making mistakes is an essential part of learning. We always have more to learn, no matter our skill level or expertise. In a climate of recipes with titles that boast of perfection and the right way or best way to execute techniques, it is hard to accept this. I don't always find comfort in the notion that perfection is unattainable and mistakes are important to our growth as humans. But being open to learning, making mistakes, and accepting that techniques evolve and recipes will evolve with them has made me a better baker. Change is the only constant; don't be afraid to be open to it.

"Failures, repeated failures, are finger posts on the road to achievement. One fails forward towards success," C. S. Lewis knowingly wrote. My recipe mess-ups didn't end with the four sunken banana bread loaves; they continued over the years. I have forgotten to put sugar in muffins and cakes. I used baking powder when I should have used baking soda. I didn't let ingredients come to room temperature as directed and made a mess of several cheesecakes. I skimmed through directions and destroyed a banana cream pie for my dad's birthday. Each time I made something that didn't turn out, with some reflection, research, or just re-reading, I was able to learn more about the ingredients and the methods used. Sometimes mistakes turned out to be treasures, like the time I accidentally cracked an extra egg into my cake batter and made the best chocolate cake of my life.

As you set out to bake from this book or other recipes you treasure and love, remember the above. Learn and embrace your mistakes; respect the recipe and the kitchen gods; be open to evolution in techniques, ingredients, and in yourself; but mostly, have fun!

HOW TO USE THIS BOOK

This book is geared toward afternoon sweets, which to me are all the baked goods that I would normally crave in the afternoon hours, complete with a cup of tea or coffee. When I learned to bake, it was always in the afternoon hours that I did so: after school with my mom, or the late-afternoon shift at the Blue Heron. There is a range of treats in these one hundred recipes, from easy to more complicated. I have purposely omitted cookies in this book since I have a whole book dedicated to them already. Most of the recipes here require basic baking

skills, such as creaming butter and adding ingredients to create a batter. A few require more of a time commitment. Be sure to follow the baking tips in the next pages and read through the lists for extra advice.

This book is divided into eight chapters. We start off in chapter 1 with One-Bowl Bakes—a chapter full of quick, delicious treats that are perfect for afternoon tea and coffee alike. There are some old stand-bys, such as Classic Birthday Cake (page 52) and Classic Crumb Cake (page 34) as well as fresh spins on classic desserts, like Maple Orange Carrot Cake (page 46) and Chocolate Red Wine Cake (page 56).

Brownies, Blondies, and Bars is the after-school/after-work chapter dreams are made of, and you will want to have a pan of Scotcharoo Blondies (page 78) and Toasted Sesame Blondies (page 81) waiting for hungry teens and tweens when the school bell rings. I've also revamped my favorite brownie recipe to make Brownies 2.0 (page 64), an even richer, chocolatey-er version of the original, which are exactly what is needed after a long day of work.

Pie Bakes are third on the list, and you'll find a range of recipes from Mixed Berry Cheesecake Slab Pie (page 121) and Millionaire Pie (page 105) to Smoky Butterscotch Cream Pie (page 112) and Lemon White Chocolate Pie (page 114). These recipes are great for afternoon entertaining.

No Bakes follow, a chapter perfect for days that shouldn't require an oven. There are some great frozen treats, such as Pumpkin Caramel

Ice Cream Cake (page 143) and Strawberry Balsamic Shortcake Ice Cream Bars (page 145), but also S'mores Bars (page 159) and Chocolate Cheesecake (page 154).

Chapter 5 is centered around feeding a large group (twenty to forty people), and contains some of my most favorite recipes. It's a chapter perfect for potlucks, wedding showers, neighborhood get-togethers, and the like. Raspberry Almond Coffee Cake Squares (page 174) are a crowd-pleaser, and Rocky Road Brownies (page 172) are an indulgent, delicious treat. Blueberry Crumble Bars (page 178) and Pretzel Shortbread Fingers (page 190) are an ideal treat for a coffee break.

The recipes in chapter 6 are perfect Weekend Projects and will require more of your time. Orange-Cinnamon Swirl Cake (page 202) is a family favorite, and Hazelnut Frangipane Cake (page 207) steals the show. The Chocolate Chip Buttermilk Cake (page 218) may just get you a marriage proposal, and the Apricot Almond Croissant (page 234) is what every lazy Sunday afternoon needs.

Chapter 7 houses all the Beginnings and Ends to the recipes: buttercreams, icings, and crusts. There are many, many variations included so you can mix and match recipes to your heart's content.

And as always, the last chapter is filled with Extras, with plenty of options to use with recipes in this book: Caramel (page 276), Pastry Cream (page 279), No-Churn Ice Cream (page 283), and Lemon Curd (page 282), just to name a few.

A FEW IMPORTANT NOTES

GENERAL BAKING ADVICE It is vital to read the entire recipe through before beginning a baking project. It is essential to know all the ingredients, details, and timing at the start to help ensure the recipe succeeds. Once you feel confident about how a recipe works, you can then think about personalizing it.

MEASURING FLOUR Throughout this book, 1 cup of flour equals 5 oz [142 g]. This is on the higher end of the scale (1 cup of flour can range anywhere from 4 to 5 oz [115 to 142 g], depending on the baker), but I found that after weighing many cups of flour and averaging the total, mine always ended up around this number.

Because most people scoop flour differently, I highly encourage the use of a scale when measuring ingredients to get consistent results, and I have provided weight measurements for that reason.

I recommend the dip-and-sweep method for flour if you are not using a scale: Dip the measuring cup into the bag or container of flour, then pull the cup out with the flour overfilling the cup. Sweep the excess off the top with a knife to end up with a level cup of flour.

MEASURING SEMISOLIDS Yogurt, sour cream, peanut butter, pumpkin purée, and the like are all examples of semisolids: ingredients that fall somewhere between a liquid and a solid. I always measure these types of ingredients in a liquid measuring cup, which gives a little more volume than a dry measuring cup because the cup is slightly bigger. If you are not using a scale to measure these ingredients, I highly recommend using a liquid measuring cup so your baked goods will turn out correctly.

A PINCH OF SALT is called for occasionally throughout these pages. It is a little more than ⅛ teaspoon, but less than ¼ teaspoon.

EGG WASH To make an egg wash, use a fork to whisk 1 large egg, a pinch of salt, and 1 tablespoon of water together in a small bowl.

FREEZE-DRIED FRUIT I often call for freeze-dried fruit powder. I find that freeze-dried fruit really bumps up the flavor of the berries in the baked goods and also helps them retain their vibrant color. If a bite of a blueberry muffin lasts three seconds, I find that the fresh blueberries are present for up to two seconds, but the freeze-dried fruit hits in that last second and really helps the berry flavor linger. In most recipes, though, the powder is optional, and the recipes will still taste good without it. To make berry powder in a food processor, use an amount of freeze-dried berries equal to the amount of powder called for in the recipe. Pulse until the berries are broken down into a powder. You can sift the powder to get rid of seeds, if desired. Store the powder in an airtight container. The longer it is stored, the harder it gets, but it will last for a few weeks.

LINING PANS WITH PARCHMENT PAPER Lining pans with a parchment paper sling results in an easy release. Cut two pieces of parchment paper the same width as the bottom of your pan, and long enough to come up and over the sides. Spray the pan with cooking spray, then place the pieces of parchment in the pan, perpendicular to each other so each side has a bit of parchment overhang, making sure to push the sheets into the corners.

TEMPERING CHOCOLATE Tempering chocolate allows it to set properly and gives the chocolate a glossy, smooth finish. Throughout the book, I use a "cheater's method" to temper chocolate, which is to melt most of the chocolate called for, and then finely chop the few ounces of chocolate left and stir it into the melted chocolate until it is also melted so that the finished, melted chocolate ends up around 88°F [31°C]. This method isn't foolproof, but it's worked for me 99 percent of the time.

On Ovens

In his cookbook *A Jewish Baker's Pastry Secrets*, George Greenstein wrote, "Ovens are often like divas or temperamental bakers, and each has its own personality." I couldn't agree more. Ovens are the most important piece of baking equipment and can often be the source of baking issues. Most home ovens are complete with hot spots, uneven baking, broken lights, fans, and thermometers—or all of the above. These factors can, of course, cause issues when baking, and it is imperative to really get to know your oven. Take time to know your hot spots, how the temperature fluctuates, and how long your oven takes to preheat. Here are some ways to help your oven out.

BUY AN OVEN THERMOMETER Many ovens are not properly calibrated, and a wrong oven temperature can greatly affect the outcome of your baked goods. If your oven is running too hot, the outsides of your baked goods can bake more quickly than the insides, resulting in burning and undercooked centers. If it is too cold, your baked goods may not rise or brown properly. I have an inexpensive oven thermometer that I keep hanging in the middle rack of my oven so I can constantly keep an eye on the temperature inside. I also have an instant-read thermometer (the DOT Simple Alarm Thermometer by ThermoWorks) that I use to check my oven temperature once a week.

PREHEAT THE OVEN This ensures that you are placing your pan in the oven at the correct temperature. Most ovens need *at least* 30 minutes to reach the correct temperature.

ROTATE THE PAN HALFWAY THROUGH BAKING Oven walls radiate heat differently due to how they vary in thickness, as well as other factors. As noted previously, most ovens have hot spots, so shifting the pan can help with even baking. But . . .

DON'T OPEN THE DOOR TOO MANY TIMES When you open the oven door, hot air spills out, causing the oven temperature to rapidly fall. Most ovens take a while to heat back up, and this can affect baking. Clean your oven window and fix that broken light so you minimize how often you open the oven door.

The Temperature and Humidity of Your Kitchen

Humidity and temperature can greatly impact the outcome of your baked goods. If your kitchen is too hot or humid, butter can soften and melt too fast. If you've let a dough or batter sit out in a hot kitchen, the butter can also separate from the dough, resulting in streaks and uneven baking. Ingredients such as flour, sugar, salt, and baking soda all soak up humidity that lingers in the air. Over time, they will retain moisture, and this can affect the outcome of the recipe. Storing your ingredients in airtight containers will keep out moisture and help them stay fresh longer.

A too-cold kitchen can cause problems, too. Butter will take longer to come to room temperature and to cream with sugar. In all these cases, it is important to pay close attention to your environment. Which brings us to . . .

Use Your Senses

I am here to guide you as best I can through each of these recipes; however, my oven, equipment, ingredients, weather, and state of mind can and will be different than yours. External factors can influence baking, but internal factors can, too. Feeling depressed or anxious can influence your concentration and could possibly alter how you read a recipe. Because I am not there with you to guide you should any of these things occur, you need to rely on your senses. If you open the oven and the cake looks like it is browning too quickly, check to see if it should come out. If the pumpkin bread is still doughy in the middle even though the baking time has elapsed, keep it in the oven longer. Using your eyes and nose will help you recognize when your baked goods are done. Your palate and hands are also good tools.

INGREDIENTS

The following is a list of ingredients used in this book. Most of these ingredients should be available at your local grocery store, but for the few that are specialty items or hard to find, I have included a resources section at the back of the book (page 296) to help you locate them.

Just like women's pant sizes, many baking ingredients vary from one brand to the next. For example, each brand of flour labeled "all-purpose" on your grocery store shelf contains a different amount of protein, ranging from 9 to 12 percent. Flour protein levels can also vary within a brand from season to season, depending on the harvest. Butter has different levels of water and fat content, depending on the brand. And one brand of granulated sugar may be coarser or finer than the next. These differences can and do affect baking outcomes. In the ingredient categories below, I list the brands I use for many of these staple items to help you achieve similar outcomes.

Dairy + Eggs

BUTTER All the recipes in this book call for unsalted butter. If you are a fan of salted butter and decide to use it instead, you will want to use a little less salt overall in the recipe. European-style butter cannot always be swapped for regular butter; the high fat content can cause extra spreading or other problems. If European-style butter is used, it will be noted in the recipe. I do not suggest substituting oils for butter.

CREAM CHEESE I prefer Philadelphia brand cream cheese in my recipes; I find it tastes best overall and gives baked goods a "creamier" feel.

CRÈME FRAÎCHE This is a matured cream with a tangy flavor and smooth texture. It is used occasionally in this book, and there is a recipe for making it at home (page 278) in the Extras chapter. I use Vermont Creamery crème fraîche when I'm not making my own.

EGGS All the recipes here call for Grade A large eggs. In its shell, a large egg should weigh 2 oz [57 g]. For egg-rich recipes (such as Pastry Cream, page 279), I like to use local, farm-fresh eggs because they typically have beautiful, orange yolks. If the recipe calls for room-temperature eggs, you can place the eggs in a large bowl, cover them with warm water, and let them sit for 10 minutes. If you need to separate the egg whites and the yolk, it's generally easier to start with a cold egg because the yolk will be firmer.

HEAVY CREAM Look for a heavy cream that is pasteurized, not ultra-pasteurized, if possible, especially when making crème fraîche. Heavy cream is also known as double cream.

MILK I tested all the recipes in this book with whole milk unless otherwise noted. I don't recommend replacing with a lower-fat milk in most recipes, as this can change the outcome of the recipe.

Cooking Oils

CANOLA OIL Canola oil is the most common oil you'll find called for in this book, because of its neutral flavor, but grapeseed oil is another good neutral option.

OLIVE OIL Use a good-quality extra-virgin olive oil so the flavor shines in the final product.

TOASTED SESAME OIL I love the flavor of toasted sesame oil, and while it is often used in savory cooking, I think pairing it with sugar is delicious. I have a few recipes in the book that include it. I prefer toasted sesame oil over regular sesame oil; I find it has a more intense flavor that works well with sugar and vanilla.

Salt + Spices

FLEUR DE SEL This is a delicate, moist salt that is usually used for finishing dishes and treats. Because the crystals are larger, the salt takes longer to dissolve, and the taste lingers a bit longer.

SPICES Make sure your spices haven't been sitting in your cupboard for years before using them. Although they appear to last forever, they do have a shelf life and can grow stale or rancid over time. Spices retain their freshness for 6 months to a year.

TABLE SALT I use table salt rather than kosher salt in all the recipes in this book unless otherwise noted.

Sweeteners

BROWN SUGAR Light brown sugar was used for recipe testing in this book. If dark brown sugar is needed, it will be specified in the recipe.

CONFECTIONERS' SUGAR Confectioners' sugar is also known as powdered sugar and icing sugar.

CORN SYRUP Do not substitute dark corn syrup for light; it has a more robust flavor and is not a good replacement in these recipes. I only use light corn syrup for recipes in this book.

GRANULATED SUGAR Granulated sugar (also known as white sugar) was used to test all the recipes in this book. Organic sugar can be substituted, but please note that it often has a coarser grain than regular white sugar, which means it won't melt as quickly as sugar that is more finely ground. If organic sugar is preferred, it can be processed in a food processor until it is finely ground before using.

SANDING SUGAR Sanding sugar is a large crystal sugar that doesn't dissolve while baking. It is used mainly for decorating.

Flours

ALL-PURPOSE FLOUR Different brands of flours have varying levels of protein, ranging from low to high, which can result in very different outcomes when baking. I've found Gold Medal unbleached all-purpose flour to be the best option for many of the recipes in this book; I use it in all the baked goods that don't use yeast. For yeasted doughs that call for all-purpose flour, I like to use King Arthur Baking Company.

ALMOND FLOUR Almond flour is also found in most grocery stores' baking aisle or can be ordered online. Look for blanched almond flour, in which the almond skins are removed before processing.

HAZELNUT FLOUR Hazelnut flour is found in most grocery stores' baking aisles or can be ordered online. If you can't find it, you can pulse skinned hazelnuts in a food processor until they are finely ground.

Leavenings

BAKING POWDER I use nonaluminum baking powder when I bake, as brands with aluminum can give off the taste of metal. Baking powder can expire. To check if your baking powder is still potent, add a spoonful of it to a cup of hot water. If it bubbles, it is still good to use.

BAKING SODA In order for baking soda to rise, it needs to be paired with an acidic ingredient, such as buttermilk, sour cream, yogurt, vinegar, coffee, molasses, brown sugar, or pumpkin. You can check baking soda for freshness the same way you would check baking powder.

Nuts

I usually toast nuts as soon as I purchase them and then store them in the freezer, as nuts can turn rancid. To toast nuts: Position an oven rack in the middle of the oven and preheat the oven to 350°F [180°C]. Line a sheet pan with parchment paper and place the nuts in the prepared pan in a single layer. Bake for 5 to 10 minutes until the nuts darken and are fragrant. Let them

cool, then store them in a plastic freezer bag in the freezer for up to 1 month.

Chocolate

BITTERSWEET AND SEMISWEET CHOCOLATE When shopping for semisweet and bittersweet bar chocolate to use in baking, look for one that falls between 35 and 60 percent cacao, and don't use anything over 70 percent, as this can alter the taste and texture of the recipe. (*Bittersweet* and *semisweet* can be confusing terms, as both can mean chocolate with a cacao percentage of anywhere from 35 to 99 percent.) Most recipes in this book call for semisweet chocolate.

When melting chocolate, chop the bar into fine pieces. This will help the chocolate melt more quickly and evenly and will give it less opportunity to burn. Make sure there is no water in your bowl when melting, or on your knife and spatula, as contact with water can cause the chocolate to seize, turning it grainy. However, adding a tablespoon or two of hot water to the seized chocolate and then stirring it can sometimes save it.

To melt chocolate in the microwave: Place the chopped chocolate in a microwave-safe bowl and microwave the chocolate on medium for 1 minute, then stop and stir the chocolate. Continue to microwave the chocolate in 20-second intervals, stirring after each one, until the chocolate is almost completely smooth. Remove the bowl from the microwave and then stir until completely smooth.

CACAO NIBS Cacao nibs have a complex, bitter flavor and are crunchy to eat.

CHOCOLATE CHIPS Chocolate chips have less cacao than bar chocolate, which allows them to hold their shape when melted. This does mean, however, that they are not always a good substitution for bar chocolate; they will not melt as quickly or as smoothly.

CHOCOLATE WAFER COOKIES Quite a few recipes in this book use chocolate wafer cookies in a cookie-crumb base, and until recently (and throughout the recipe testing of this book) these cookies could be purchased at the grocery store. They have been discontinued, so I have included a recipe for my own version of Chocolate Wafer Cookies on page 270. Oreo Thins are also a good replacement, but their cream filling will change the taste and texture of the final crust, and you may need to add more cookie crumbs to balance the cookie-to-butter ratio.

COCOA POWDER There are two kinds of cocoa powder: Dutch-process and natural. Dutch-process cocoa is treated; it is washed with an alkaline solution that neutralizes its acids and has a more mellow, nutty flavor and a richer color. Natural cocoa powder is left as is and is a very acidic, sharp powder. The recipes in this book all call for Dutch-process cocoa powder.

WHITE CHOCOLATE White chocolate is made from cocoa butter. Not all white chocolate is created equally, so use a brand you trust when baking with it. White chocolate chips do not melt well. White chocolate also melts more quickly than dark chocolate, so be sure to stir it more frequently than you would dark chocolate, especially when using the microwave.

Vanilla

VANILLA BEANS To use a vanilla bean: Use a sharp knife to split the bean lengthwise, then scrape the seeds out of the bean with the dull side of the knife or a spoon. Use the seeds in the recipe as called for. The leftover pod can be dried and then finely ground in a food processor to make a vanilla bean powder.

VANILLA EXTRACT All the recipes in this book use pure vanilla extract, and I don't recommend using artificial vanilla, as the taste is, well, artificial.

EQUIPMENT

Measuring Equipment

DIGITAL SCALE A digital scale will ensure that ingredients are measured correctly. Throughout this book, I have weights listed for most ingredients. I have not included weights for small measurements that are less than 4 tablespoons. A digital scale can also be used for portioning out cookie dough and dividing cake batter evenly between pans.

MEASURING CUPS AND SPOONS Dry measuring cups measure dry ingredients. I use metal cups that come in these sizes: ¼ cup, ⅓ cup, ½ cup, and 1 cup. I use metal measuring spoons for teaspoon and tablespoon measures: ¼ teaspoon, ½ teaspoon, 1 teaspoon, and 1 tablespoon. For liquids, I use glass measuring cups with pourable spouts and measurements marked along the side of the cup.

Utensils

BAKING PANS I call for a few baking pans in this book: a 9 by 13 in [23 by 33 cm] pan, a 9 in [23 cm] circle pan, 8 in [20 cm] circle and square pans, a 10 in [25 cm] square pan, and 8 in [20 cm] and 9 in [23 cm] circle springform pans. A 9 in [23 cm] square pan can be substituted for the latter pan, but the higher sides help make a nice, tall bake in some recipes. Avoid glass pans and dark or black nonstick coatings, as they tend to overbrown recipes.

BENCH SCRAPER A bench scraper is a great tool used for so many things, from transferring ingredients to lifting dough off the counter, cutting dough, and cleaning the work surface.

FOOD PROCESSOR I use a food processor for pulverizing nuts and grating carrots quickly.

HEAVY-DUTY STAND MIXER If you do a lot of baking, I highly recommend investing in a stand mixer for both convenience and speed. The recipes in this book call for one, but a hand-held mixer or sturdy wooden spoon can be substituted.

INSTANT-READ THERMOMETER An instant-read thermometer is an essential tool and is especially useful when making caramel. As its name suggests, it tells the temperature instantly, so you have a better chance of making your confections perfectly.

KITCHEN SCISSORS Kitchen scissors have many functions, like cutting parchment paper and pastry bag tips, as well as snipping dough.

KITCHEN TORCH I use my kitchen torch to caramelize sugar, brown meringues, and toast marshmallows.

MICROWAVE OVEN A microwave oven is a useful alternative to a double boiler for melting butter and chocolate, and also works well to heat milk.

OFFSET SPATULA Offset spatulas are used for spreading batter evenly and icing cookies and cakes. I use both large and small ones, and prefer them with a rounded edge over a straight edge.

OVEN THERMOMETER Many ovens are not properly calibrated, and this can greatly affect the outcome of your baked good. I have an inexpensive oven thermometer that I keep hanging on the middle rack of my oven.

PARCHMENT PAPER I use parchment paper for lining sheet pans when baking, and I use it as a sling when making quick breads and bars for easy removal. I like to buy parchment paper from a restaurant supply store, where the sheets come precut and lay flat.

PASTRY BRUSHES Pastry brushes have so many uses—glazing, coating, and brushing away crumbs and excess flour. I use a natural-bristle brush; I've found they work much better than silicone, although they need to be replaced more frequently.

PORTION SCOOP Portion scoops are a great way to scoop batter, helping ensure consistent and even shapes. They are not essential, but I highly recommend them. Vollrath makes a reliable scoop that doesn't break easily.

RULER Rulers are useful for measuring when cutting dough. I have an 18 in [46 cm] long ruler that works perfectly.

SHEET PAN I use medium-weight half sheet pans (12 by 16 in [30.5 by 40.5 cm] with a 1 in [2.5 cm] rim), unless otherwise noted.

SILICONE SPATULA Spatulas are an essential kitchen tool with many uses: folding, smoothing, stirring, mixing, and scraping, just to name a few.

SKEWERS I use wooden skewers for testing when bars and brownies are done. A toothpick can also be used.

WIRE COOLING RACK Cooling racks help the bottom of baked goods stay crisp, and also help speed up cooling times.

WIRE WHISK I use whisks for many kitchen tasks, such as beating eggs and combining dry ingredients.

ZESTER A Microplane zester comes in handy when a recipe calls for freshly grated nutmeg or gingerroot, or the zest of an orange or lemon.

One-Bowl Bakes

"**Our life is** frittered away **by detail. . . .** Simplify, **simplify."**

—Henry David Thoreau, *Walden and Other Writings*

Over the years, I have made many so-called snacking cakes, and while they were all delicious, not one was the cake I was searching for. By *afternoon snacking cake*, I don't mean a single-layer chocolate or yellow cake smothered in frosting. I mean a moist, flavorful, straight-up cake with a crunchy, sugary top. A cake that doesn't need icing, or fruit, or streusel but is perfect straight from the pan. A cake with a tender base and a delicate, but substantial, crumb. This cake doesn't need anything extra, truly. I love it just warm to the touch with a steaming cup of coffee.

My Perfect Afternoon Snacking Cake

MAKES · 9 LARGE OR 12 SMALL SQUARES

4 tablespoons [56 g] unsalted butter, melted and cooled

1½ cups [300 g] granulated sugar, plus 3 tablespoons for sprinkling

¾ cup [168 g] olive oil

¾ cup [180 g] buttermilk, at room temperature

3 large eggs, at room temperature

1 tablespoon orange zest

1 tablespoon triple sec or other orange liqueur

1 teaspoon pure vanilla extract

1 teaspoon salt

¾ teaspoon baking powder

½ teaspoon baking soda

2 cups [284 g] all-purpose flour

1) Position an oven rack in the middle of the oven and preheat the oven to 350°F [180°C]. Grease a 9 in [23 cm] square baking pan and line with a parchment sling. 2) In a large bowl, whisk together the melted butter, 1½ cups [300 g] of the granulated sugar, the olive oil, buttermilk, eggs, zest, triple sec, vanilla, salt, baking powder, and baking soda. Add the flour and stir with a spatula until just combined. Switch to a whisk and whisk the batter to eliminate any remaining flour lumps, about 10 seconds. 3) Pour the batter into the prepared pan. Sprinkle the top of the cake evenly with the remaining 3 tablespoons of sugar. 4) Bake for 24 to 32 minutes, rotating the pan halfway through, until the top is golden brown and a wooden skewer or toothpick inserted into the center comes out clean. Transfer

the pan to a wire rack and let cool for 20 minutes, then use the parchment sling to remove the
cake from the pan. Cut into squares and serve
just warm to the touch. The cake can be stored
in an airtight container at room temperature for
up to 3 days.

1

This is a joyful little cake, bursting with color and flavor. My kids ask for this topped with strawberry buttercream, but I prefer raspberry, as it has a little more bite and balances the sweetness from the sprinkles. Both are delicious, however, and perfect for afternoon snacking.

Confetti Cake
with Berry Buttercream

MAKES · 12 LARGE OR
24 SMALL SQUARES

12 tablespoons [1½ sticks or 170 g] unsalted butter, melted and cooled

2 cups [400 g] granulated sugar

Scant 1 cup [210 g] egg whites (from 6 or 7 large eggs), at room temperature

1 cup [240 g] milk, at room temperature

½ cup [120 g] Crème Fraîche (page 278) or sour cream, at room temperature

¼ cup [56 g] vegetable or canola oil

1 tablespoon pure vanilla extract

4 teaspoons baking powder

1 teaspoon salt

2¾ cups [391 g] all-purpose flour

¾ cup [115 g] sprinkles

1 recipe American Buttercream, raspberry variation (page 245)

1) Position an oven rack in the middle of the oven and preheat the oven to 350°F [180°C]. Grease a 9 by 13 in [23 by 33 cm] baking pan and line with a parchment sling. 2) In a large bowl, whisk together the melted butter, granulated sugar, egg whites, milk, crème fraîche, oil, vanilla, baking powder, and salt. Add the flour and use a spatula to stir it into the batter. Switch to a whisk and whisk the batter to eliminate any remaining flour lumps, about 10 seconds. Add the sprinkles and mix again with the spatula until just combined. 3) Pour the batter into the prepared pan and use an offset spatula to smooth the top. Tap the pan on the counter twice to get rid of any air bubbles.

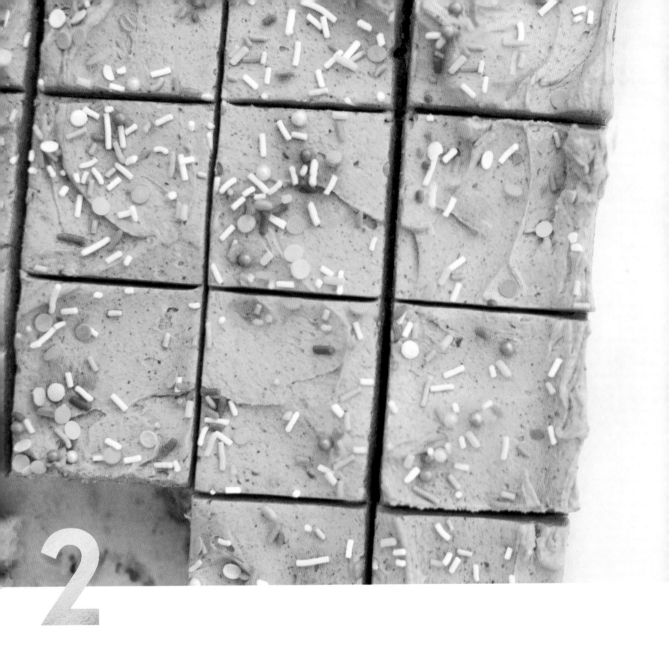

2

4) Bake for 24 to 32 minutes, rotating the pan halfway through, until a wooden skewer or toothpick inserted into the center comes out clean. Transfer the pan to a wire rack and let the cake cool for 20 minutes in the pan, then use the parchment sling to remove the cake and let it finish cooling on the wire rack before icing. Top the cake evenly with the buttercream, decorate as desired, then slice into squares and serve. The cake can be stored in the refrigerator, covered, for up to 2 days.

Back in my coffeehouse baking days, we often made a classic crumb cake to grace the bake case. It was a rich, dense cake layer topped with piles of streusel and dusted with confectioners' sugar. I've kept the basic principles of that cake, but I add a little more salt to the crumb topping to help tame the sweetness. Confectioners' sugar isn't necessary on top but sure does look pretty.

Classic Crumb Cake

MAKES · 12 LARGE OR
24 SMALL SQUARES

CRUMB TOPPING

2½ cups [355 g] all-purpose flour

1 cup [200 g] brown sugar

4 teaspoons ground cinnamon

¾ teaspoon salt

1½ cups [3 sticks or 339 g] unsalted butter, at room temperature

CAKE

10 tablespoons [140 g] unsalted butter, melted and cooled

1¾ cups [350 g] granulated sugar

Scant ¾ cup [175 g] egg whites (from 5 or 6 large eggs), at room temperature

¾ cup [180 g] sour cream, at room temperature

¼ cup [56 g] vegetable or canola oil

1 tablespoon pure vanilla extract

1 tablespoon cornstarch

1 tablespoon baking powder

1 teaspoon salt

2⅓ cups [331 g] all-purpose flour

Confectioners' sugar, for dusting (optional)

1) **FOR THE CRUMB TOPPING** In the bowl of a stand mixer fitted with a paddle, combine the flour, brown sugar, cinnamon, and salt. Add the butter and mix on low speed until large clumps of streusel form. The topping can be used immediately or refrigerated for up to 1 week. 2) **FOR THE CAKE** Position an oven rack in the middle of the oven and preheat the oven to 350°F [180°C]. Grease a 9 by 13 in [23 by 33 cm] baking pan and line with a parchment sling. In a large bowl, whisk together the melted butter, granulated sugar, egg whites, sour cream, oil, vanilla, cornstarch, baking powder, and salt. Add the flour and use a spatula to stir it into the batter. Switch to a whisk and whisk the batter to eliminate any remaining flour lumps, about 10 seconds. Pour the batter into the prepared pan and use an offset

spatula to smooth the top. Sprinkle the streusel evenly over the cake batter. Tap the pan on the counter twice to help get rid of any air bubbles. 3) Bake for 35 to 50 minutes, rotating the pan halfway through, until the streusel is golden brown and a wooden skewer or toothpick inserted into the center of the cake comes out clean. Transfer the cake in the pan to a wire rack and let cool for 20 minutes.

4) Remove the cake from the pan using the parchment sling, then let cool until just warm to the touch. Before serving, dust the cake with confectioners' sugar, if using. The cake can be stored in an airtight container at room temperature for up to 3 days.

3

My children are the reason for this cake: Both prefer a plain, unfrosted, single-layer yellow cake over any other kind—their ideal after-school snack. And after tasting this cake, warm to the touch with just a simple dusting of confectioners' sugar, I have to say that they make a very compelling argument (although I'm not ready to give up buttercream just yet).

Straight-Up Yellow Snacking Cake

MAKES · 9 LARGE
OR 12 SMALL SQUARES

8 tablespoons [1 stick or 113 g] unsalted butter, melted and cooled

1¾ cups [350 g] granulated sugar

½ cup [120 g] buttermilk

⅓ cup [75 g] vegetable or canola oil

1 teaspoon salt

½ teaspoon baking powder

¼ teaspoon baking soda

2¼ cups [320 g] all-purpose flour

Confectioners' sugar, for dusting

1) Position an oven rack in the middle of the oven and preheat the oven to 350°F [180°C]. Grease a 10 in [25 cm] or 9 in [23 cm] square baking pan and line with a parchment sling. 2) In a large bowl, whisk together the melted butter, granulated sugar, butter-milk, oil, salt, baking powder, and baking soda. Add the flour and use a spatula to stir it into the batter. Switch to a whisk and whisk the batter to eliminate any remaining flour lumps, about 10 seconds. Pour the batter into the prepared pan and use an offset spatula to smooth the top. Tap the pan gently on the counter twice to help get rid of any air bubbles.

3) Bake for 42 to 50 minutes, rotating the pan halfway through, until the cake is golden brown and a wooden skewer or toothpick inserted into the center comes out clean. Transfer the pan to a wire rack and let cool for 20 minutes. Use the parchment sling to remove the cake from the pan, move to the wire rack, and then let cool completely. Dust the cake with confectioners' sugar. Cut the cake into squares and serve. The cake can be stored in an airtight container at room temperature for up to 3 days.

This little cake is bursting with flavor: The base is lemony with a scattering of poppy seeds, and the raspberry icing adds both a bright color and intense flavor. I find myself making this in February and early March, when it snows forever here in the North with no end in sight, and I'm looking for a sign of Aslan's return. The pretty pink icing cheers the heart right up, and the burst of lemon awakens a hibernating soul.

Raspberry Poppy Seed Cake

MAKES · 9 LARGE OR 12 SMALL SQUARES

CAKE

10 tablespoons [140 g] unsalted butter, melted and cooled

1½ cups [300 g] granulated sugar

¾ cup [180 g] buttermilk, at room temperature

3 large eggs, at room temperature

¼ cup [60 g] lemon juice

2 tablespoons vegetable or canola oil

1 tablespoon poppy seeds

1 teaspoon pure vanilla extract

1 teaspoon baking powder

¾ teaspoon salt

¼ teaspoon baking soda

2 cups [284 g] all-purpose flour

RASPBERRY GLAZE

¼ cup [16 g] freeze-dried raspberry powder (see page 16)

2 tablespoons unsalted butter, melted

2 to 4 tablespoons lemon juice

Pinch of salt

1½ cups [180 g] confectioners' sugar

1) FOR THE CAKE Position an oven rack in the middle of the oven and preheat the oven to 350°F [180°C]. Grease a 8 in [20 cm] or 9 in [23 cm] square baking pan and line with a parchment sling. 2) In a large bowl, whisk together the melted butter, granulated sugar, buttermilk, eggs, lemon juice, oil, poppy seeds, vanilla, baking powder, salt, and baking soda. Add the flour and use a spatula to stir it into the batter. Switch to a whisk and whisk the batter to eliminate any remaining flour lumps, about 10 seconds. 3) Pour the batter into the prepared pan and use an offset spatula to smooth the top. Tap the pan gently on the counter twice to help get rid of any air bubbles.

4) Bake until the cake is golden brown and a wooden skewer or toothpick inserted into the center comes out clean, rotating the pan halfway through, 32 to 40 minutes. 5) FOR THE RASPBERRY GLAZE In a medium bowl, combine the freeze-dried raspberry powder, melted butter, 2 tablespoons of the lemon juice, and the salt. Add the confectioners' sugar and use a spatula to combine, then whisk until smooth. Add more lemon juice, 1 tablespoon at a time, until the glaze is thick but pourable. 6) Transfer the pan to a wire rack and let cool for 5 minutes. Pour the glaze over the warm cake and let sit until the glaze is set. Use the parchment sling to remove the cake from the pan, transfer it to the wire rack, and let cool completely. Cut the cake into squares and serve. The cake can be stored in an airtight container at room temperature for up to 3 days.

5

Upside-down cakes: What a glorious thing they are when they work! But, as I know from experience, turning over the hot pan onto a serving plate can lead to a capsize rather than a gentle flip. I've found lining the pan with parchment helps quite a bit, and berries can easily be pushed back into place if they don't stay put during their journey. Cranberries and caramel are a good pair, as the tart balances out the sweet (sour cherries also work well). A hefty dollop of whipped cream is also highly encouraged.

Cranberry Caramel Upside-Down Cake

MAKES · ONE 9 IN [23 CM] CAKE

CAKE
¾ cup [170 g] vegetable or canola oil

1½ cups [300 g] granulated sugar, plus more for sprinkling

3 large eggs, at room temperature

½ cup [120 g] sour cream, at room temperature

2 tablespoons lemon juice

1 tablespoon pure vanilla extract

½ teaspoon baking powder

¾ teaspoon salt

¼ teaspoon baking soda

1¾ cups [250 g] all-purpose flour

CRANBERRY CARAMEL TOPPING
5 tablespoons [70 g] unsalted butter, at room temperature

⅓ cup [65 g] granulated sugar

⅓ cup [65 g] brown sugar

Pinch of salt

3 cups [300 g] fresh cranberries

1 recipe Whipped Cream (page 278), optional

1) FOR THE CAKE Position an oven rack in the middle of the oven and preheat the oven to 350°F [180°C]. Grease a 9 in [23 cm] springform baking pan and line the bottom with parchment. 2) In a large bowl, whisk together the oil, granulated sugar, eggs, sour cream, lemon juice, vanilla, baking powder, salt, and baking soda. Add the flour and use a spatula to stir it into the batter. Switch to a whisk and whisk the batter to eliminate any remaining flour lumps, about 10 seconds. 3) FOR THE CRANBERRY CARAMEL TOPPING Place the butter in the prepared pan and place it in the oven until the butter melts, 3 to 4 minutes. Carefully remove the pan and add the granulated and brown sugars and the salt, using a

spatula to combine it into the butter. Place the pan back in the oven and let the mixture bake until the sugar has dissolved and is starting to bubble, 3 to 4 minutes. Remove from the oven and scatter the cranberries over the top of the sugar mixture. 4) Immediately pour the cake batter over the top of the cranberries, using an offset spatula to smooth the top. Tap the pan twice on the counter to help get rid of any air bubbles. 5) Return the pan to the oven and bake for 55 to 70 minutes, until a wooden skewer or toothpick inserted into the center comes out clean. 6) Let the cake cool in the pan for 5 minutes, then carefully run an offset spatula or butter knife around the edges of the pan to gently loosen the cake from the sides. Invert the cake onto a serving plate and carefully peel off the parchment paper. If any cranberries stick to the parchment, carefully place them back on the cake. Serve the cake just warm to the touch, with a dollop of whipped cream (if using). The cake is best eaten the same day it is made.

Readers often message me to let me know how they have tweaked my recipes, which sometimes involves baking them in different vessels than my recipe calls for. Muffin batter is one of these recipes that works well with this adaptation. I decided to play along and baked my favorite Blueberry Muffin recipe in a cake pan. Now, not only do I get to skip scrubbing out a muffin pan, but I also have a perfect way to sneak morning muffins into the afternoon hours. A healthy dusting of sugar and a grating of nutmeg on the top make this snacking cake perfection.

MAKES · 9 LARGE OR 12 SMALL SQUARES

Blueberry Muffin Cake

5 tablespoons [70 g] unsalted butter, melted and cooled

1 cup [200 g] granulated sugar, plus more for sprinkling

¾ cup [180 g] buttermilk, at room temperature

½ cup [50 g] almond flour

⅓ cup [75 g] vegetable or canola oil

¼ cup [60 g] sour cream, at room temperature

2 large eggs, at room temperature

1 tablespoon lemon juice

2 teaspoons baking powder

1 teaspoon salt

1 teaspoon pure vanilla extract

1 teaspoon lemon zest

¼ teaspoon baking soda

2 cups [284 g] all-purpose flour

6 oz [170 g] fresh or frozen blueberries, chopped into bite-size pieces

½ teaspoon freshly grated nutmeg

1) Position an oven rack in the middle of the oven and preheat the oven to 350°F [180°C]. Grease a 9 in [23 cm] square baking pan and line with a parchment sling. 2) In a large bowl, whisk together the melted butter, granulated sugar, buttermilk, almond flour, oil, sour cream, eggs, lemon juice, baking powder, salt, vanilla, lemon zest, and baking soda until completely combined. Add the all-purpose flour and use a spatula to gently mix until almost combined. Fold in the blueberries until just incorporated, being careful not to overwork the batter. It should not be completely smooth; there should be some visible lumps and bumps. 3) Pour the batter into the prepared pan and smooth the top with the back of a spoon or an offset spatula. Generously sprinkle granulated sugar evenly over the top of the batter. 4) Bake for 42 to 50 minutes, rotating the pan halfway through, until the top of the cake is golden brown and a wooden skewer or toothpick inserted into the center of the cake comes out with the slightest hint of crumb. Transfer the pan to a wire rack and sprinkle the nutmeg over the top of the cake. Let cool until just warm to the touch. Use the parchment sling to remove the cake, then cut into squares and serve. The cake is best eaten the same day it is made, but can be stored in an airtight container at room temperature for up to 2 days.

7

My love for banana bread is strong, and while I usually partake of it in loaf form, I'm rather smitten with this cake version, complete with cream cheese buttercream. This banana cake is perfectly moist, and the tang in the icing is a perfect complement. Topping this cake with Fudge Buttercream (page 256) would also be a good idea.

Banana Bread Bars

MAKES · 9 LARGE OR 12 SMALL SQUARES

5 tablespoons [70 g] unsalted butter

1 cup [227 g] mashed, very ripe bananas (about 3 bananas)

½ cup [100 g] granulated sugar

½ cup [100 g] brown sugar

⅓ cup [80 g] buttermilk, at room temperature

¼ cup [60 g] vegetable or canola oil

1 tablespoon pure vanilla extract

1 teaspoon salt

2 large eggs, at room temperature

1 teaspoon baking soda

1½ cups [213 g] all-purpose flour

1 recipe Cream Cheese Buttercream (page 250)

1) Position an oven rack in the middle of the oven and preheat the oven to 350°F [180°C]. Grease an 8 in [20 cm] square baking pan and line with a parchment sling. 2) In a large, heavy-bottom saucepan set over medium-high heat, brown the butter until golden (for tips on browning butter, see page 276). Whisk in the bananas, then follow with the granulated and brown sugars, buttermilk, oil, vanilla, and salt. Let the mixture cool to room temperature. Add the eggs and whisk until completely combined. Add the baking soda and whisk again, then add the flour and stir with a spatula until just combined. 3) Pour the batter into the prepared pan and use the back of a spoon or an offset spatula to smooth the top. Bake, rotating the pan halfway through, until the top of the cake

is golden and a wooden skewer or toothpick inserted into the center comes out clean, 30 to 35 minutes. Let the cake cool for 20 minutes in the pan, then use the parchment sling to remove the cake and let it finish cooling before icing. Top the cake evenly with the buttercream, then slice into squares and serve. The cake can be stored in the refrigerator, covered, for up to 2 days.

VARIATION

• **Banana Bread Cake with Streusel:** *After adding the batter to the pan, evenly sprinkle the top of the cake with 1½ cups [220 g] Pecan Streusel (page 287). Bake as directed. Omit the cream cheese buttercream.*

Carrot cake was my go-to cake in college when I was trying to make a good impression; I made several for my husband while we were dating and brought one to every wedding shower I hosted. This version is a single-layer affair, but orange liqueur and maple cream cheese make this even more sophisticated and delicious than the classic two-layer cake. Add some piped meringue and a touch of gold leaf, and your afternoon is officially elevated.

Maple Orange Carrot Cake

MAKES · 9 LARGE OR 12 SMALL SQUARES

CAKE

⅔ cup [150 g] vegetable oil

¾ cup [150 g] granulated sugar

¼ cup [50 g] brown sugar

2 large eggs, at room temperature

1 tablespoon orange zest

1 tablespoon triple sec

1 teaspoon ground cinnamon

1 teaspoon ground ginger

¾ teaspoon baking powder

½ teaspoon baking soda

½ teaspoon salt

Pinch of ground cloves

1½ cups [213 g] all-purpose flour

2 cups [200 g] finely grated carrots

MAPLE CREAM CHEESE ICING

2 oz [57 g] cream cheese, at room temperature

4 tablespoons [56 g] unsalted butter, at room temperature

¼ teaspoon salt

¼ cup [80 g] maple syrup

1 teaspoon pure vanilla extract

1 cup [120 g] confectioners' sugar

1) FOR THE CAKE Position an oven rack in the middle of the oven and preheat the oven to 350°F [180°C]. Grease an 8 in [20 cm] square baking pan and line with a parchment sling. 2) In a large bowl, whisk together the oil, granulated and brown sugars, eggs, orange zest, triple sec, cinnamon, ginger, baking powder, baking soda, salt, and cloves until completely combined. Add the flour, stirring with a spatula until just combined, then add the carrots, stirring until incorporated. 3) Pour the batter into the prepared pan and use the back of a spoon or an offset spatula to smooth the top. 4) Bake for 30 to 35 minutes, rotating the pan halfway through, until a wooden skewer or toothpick inserted into the center of the cake comes out clean. Let the cake cool for 20 minutes in the pan, then use the parchment sling to remove the cake and let it finish cooling before icing.

5) FOR THE MAPLE CREAM CHEESE ICING In the bowl of a stand mixer fitted with a paddle, beat the cream cheese, butter, and salt on low speed for 2 to 3 minutes until smooth, creamy, and combined. Scrape down the bowl, add the maple syrup and vanilla, and mix again on low speed until completely combined. Gradually add the confectioners' sugar and mix on low speed until combined and smooth, scraping down the sides of the bowl as necessary. Top the cake evenly with the icing, then slice into squares and serve. The cake can be stored in the refrigerator, covered, for up to 2 days.

VARIATION

• **Showstopper Carrot Cake:** *Add meringue to the top of the cake: Bake and frost the cake as directed, then chill in the refrigerator for 1 hour. Make the Meringue as directed on page 258, then, working quickly, place the meringue mixture into a pastry bag fitted with a ½ in [13 mm] plain tip. Pipe meringue kisses over the top of the buttercream.*

9

"Because although Eating Honey *was* a very good thing to do, there was a moment just before you began to eat it which was better than when you were, but he didn't know what it was called." Winnie the Pooh was on to something with his honey obsession, and this cake will evoke the same simple pleasure. The honey gives the cake a subtle richness that is particularly tasty paired with sesame.

Honey Sesame Cake

MAKES · ONE 8 IN
[20 CM] CAKE

8 tablespoons [1 stick or 113 g] unsalted butter, melted and cooled

¾ cup [150 g] granulated sugar

¼ cup [85 g] honey

2 large eggs, at room temperature

½ cup [120 g] buttermilk, at room temperature

1 tablespoon pure vanilla extract

1 teaspoon toasted sesame oil

¾ teaspoon baking powder

½ teaspoon baking soda

½ teaspoon salt

1¼ cups [178 g] all-purpose flour

1 recipe Ganache (page 257)

1) Position an oven rack in the middle of the oven and preheat the oven to 350°F [180°C]. Grease an 8 in [20 cm] baking pan and line the bottom with parchment.
2) In a large bowl, whisk together the butter, granulated sugar, honey, eggs, buttermilk, vanilla, toasted sesame oil, baking powder, baking soda, and salt. Add the flour and use a spatula to combine it into the batter. Switch to a whisk and whisk the batter to eliminate any remaining flour lumps, about 10 seconds. 3) Pour the batter into the prepared pan and use an offset spatula to smooth the top. Tap the pan on the counter twice to help get rid of any air bubbles.

4) Bake for 32 to 45 minutes, rotating the pan halfway through, until a wooden skewer or toothpick inserted into the center comes out clean. Transfer the pan to a wire rack and let the cake cool for 20 minutes in the pan, then invert the cake onto a wire rack set over a baking sheet. Top the cake with the ganache and let cool to room temperature. Slice and serve. The cake can be stored in an airtight container in the refrigerator for up to 2 days.

Although this doughnut cake is not actually fried, it does capture the flavors of an old-fashioned yeasted doughnut with the tangy flavor of buttermilk and crème fraîche, along with vanilla and a hefty sprinkling of cinnamon sugar. It's afternoon comfort at its finest and hits the spot paired with coffee or tea.

Jam-Filled Doughnut Cake

MAKES · 9 LARGE OR
12 SMALL SQUARES

TOPPING

3 tablespoons granulated sugar

1 teaspoon ground cinnamon

CAKE

4 tablespoons [56 g] unsalted butter, melted and cooled

1 cup [200 g] granulated sugar

½ cup [120 g] buttermilk, at room temperature

½ cup [120 g] Crème Fraîche (page 278) or sour cream, at room temperature

¼ cup [56 g] vegetable or canola oil

2 large eggs, at room temperature

1 tablespoon pure vanilla extract

2 teaspoons baking powder

¾ teaspoon salt

⅛ teaspoon baking soda

2 cups [284 g] all-purpose flour

½ cup [112 g] raspberry or apricot jam

11

1) FOR THE TOPPING In a small bowl, combine the granulated sugar and cinnamon. Set aside.

2) FOR THE CAKE Position an oven rack in the middle of the oven and preheat the oven to 350°F [180°C]. Grease an 8 in [20 cm] square baking pan and line with a parchment sling.

3) In a large bowl, whisk together the melted butter, granulated sugar, buttermilk, crème fraîche, oil, eggs, vanilla, baking powder, salt, and baking soda. Add the flour and mix with a rubber spatula until combined. Switch to a whisk and whisk the batter to eliminate any remaining flour lumps, about 10 seconds.

4) Pour half of the batter into the prepared pan. Pour the jam on top and use the back of a spoon to evenly spread it across the batter. Top with the remaining batter and use an offset spatula or the back of a spoon to smooth the top. Sprinkle the topping over the batter.

5) Bake for 24 to 30 minutes, rotating the pan halfway through, until a wooden skewer or toothpick inserted into the center comes out clean. Let the cake cool for 20 minutes in the pan, then use the parchment sling to remove the cake and let it finish cooling. Slice into squares and serve. Store the cake in an airtight container at room temperature for up to 2 days.

This is my best yellow cake. I spent several years tinkering with the recipe, finally succeeding at creating a cake that is rich and moist and bakes up beautifully. I found the addition of almond flour to be the trick; it keeps the crumb tender over several days. In my original recipe I use the reverse creaming method to add the butter to the cake, but I found that using melted butter (and making this a one-bowl affair) also works great. Any of the other buttercreams in chapter 7 are tasty paired with this base, but the Fudge Buttercream, page 256, is a birthday classic.

Classic Birthday Cake

MAKES · 12 LARGE OR 24 SMALL SQUARES

12 tablespoons [1½ sticks or 170 g] unsalted butter, melted and cooled

2 cups [400 g] granulated sugar

4 large eggs, at room temperature

2 large egg yolks, at room temperature

¾ cup [180 g] buttermilk, at room temperature

½ cup [120 g] sour cream, at room temperature

½ cup [50 g] almond flour

¼ cup [56 g] vegetable or canola oil

1 tablespoon pure vanilla extract

2 teaspoons baking powder

1¼ teaspoons salt

½ teaspoon baking soda

2⅓ cups [331 g] all-purpose flour

1 recipe Fudge Buttercream (page 256)

12

1) Position an oven rack in the middle of the oven and preheat the oven to 350°F [180°C]. Grease a 9 by 13 in [23 by 33 cm] baking pan and line with a parchment sling. 2) In a large bowl, whisk together the melted butter, granulated sugar, eggs, egg yolks, buttermilk, sour cream, almond flour, oil, vanilla, baking powder, salt, and baking soda. Add the all-purpose flour and use a spatula to stir it into the batter. Switch to a whisk and whisk the batter to eliminate any remaining flour lumps, about 10 seconds. 3) Pour the batter into the prepared pan and use an offset spatula to smooth the top. Tap the pan on the counter twice to get rid of any air bubbles. 4) Bake for 32 to 40 minutes, rotating the pan halfway through, until a wooden skewer or toothpick inserted into the center comes out clean.

Let the cake cool for 20 minutes in the pan,
then use the parchment sling to remove the
cake and let it finish cooling before icing. Top
the cake evenly with the buttercream, decorate
as desired, then slice into squares and serve.
Store the cake in the refrigerator, covered,
for up to 2 days.

This recipe was tested during my kids' continuous *Monty Python and the Holy Grail* viewing phase, and I wonder if perhaps King Arthur's empty clanging coconut shells pricked my subconscious, drawing me to these flavors. With coconut milk in both the cake and the icing, and a delicate speckling of chocolate chips, I am certain even the Black Knight would let me pass if I offered him a slice.

Coconut Chocolate Chip Cake

MAKES · 12 LARGE OR 24 SMALL SQUARES

10 tablespoons [140 g] unsalted butter, melted and cooled

1¾ cups [350 g] granulated sugar

Scant ¾ cup [175 g] egg whites (from 5 or 6 large eggs), at room temperature

½ cup [120 g] coconut milk, at room temperature

⅓ cup [80 g] sour cream, at room temperature

¼ cup [56 g] vegetable or canola oil

1 tablespoon cornstarch

1 tablespoon baking powder

2 teaspoons coconut extract

1 teaspoon pure vanilla extract

1 teaspoon salt

2⅓ cups [331 g] all-purpose flour

¾ cup [128 g] mini semisweet chocolate chips

1 recipe Ermine Buttercream (page 246), coconut variation

Coconut flakes, for sprinkling

1) Position an oven rack in the middle of the oven and preheat the oven to 350°F [180°C]. Grease a 9 by 13 in [23 by 33 cm] baking pan and line with a parchment sling. 2) In a large bowl, whisk together the melted butter, granulated sugar, egg whites, coconut milk, sour cream, oil, cornstarch, baking powder, coconut extract, vanilla, and salt. Add the flour and use a spatula to stir it into the batter. Switch to a whisk and whisk the batter to eliminate any remaining flour lumps, about 10 seconds. Stir in the mini chocolate chips. 3) Pour the batter into the prepared pan and use an offset spatula to smooth the top. Tap the pan on the counter twice to get rid of any air bubbles.

13

4) Bake for 24 to 32 minutes, rotating the pan halfway through, until a wooden skewer or toothpick inserted into the center comes out clean. Let the cake cool for 20 minutes in the pan, then use the parchment sling to remove the cake and let it finish cooling before icing. Top the cake evenly with the buttercream, sprinkle with coconut flakes, then slice into squares and serve. Store the cake in the refrigerator, covered, for up to 2 days.

"If we sip the wine, we find dreams coming upon us out of the imminent night," D. H. Lawrence astutely observed, and I wonder if he'd feel the same if he snacked the wine instead of sipped. I certainly do. This cake boasts red wine flavor, along with a bit of chocolate. It's delicious with cream cheese frosting, but you could also dust cocoa powder over the top for a simpler option. Either way, you'll find it's what sweet dreams are made of.

MAKES · 12 LARGE
OR 24 SMALL
SQUARES

Chocolate Red Wine Cake

8 tablespoons [1 stick or 113 g] unsalted butter, melted and cooled

2 cups [400 g] granulated sugar

3 large eggs, at room temperature

¾ cup [180 g] buttermilk, at room temperature

½ cup [120 g] red wine, preferably Merlot

½ cup [112 g] vegetable or canola oil

½ cup [50 g] Dutch-process cocoa powder

2 teaspoons baking powder

1¼ teaspoons salt

1 teaspoon pure vanilla extract

½ teaspoon baking soda

2⅓ cups [331 g] all-purpose flour

1 recipe Cream Cheese Buttercream (page 250)

14

1) Position an oven rack in the middle of the oven and preheat the oven to 350°F [180°C]. Grease a 9 by 13 in [23 by 33 cm] baking pan and line with a parchment sling. 2) In a large bowl, whisk together the melted butter, granulated sugar, eggs, buttermilk, red wine, oil, cocoa powder, baking powder, salt, vanilla, and baking soda. Add the flour and use a spatula to stir it into the batter. Switch to a whisk and whisk the batter to eliminate any remaining flour lumps, about 10 seconds. 3) Pour the batter into the prepared pan and use an offset spatula to smooth the top. Tap the pan gently on the counter twice to help get rid of any air bubbles.

4) Bake for 32 to 36 minutes, rotating the pan halfway through, until the cake is golden brown and a wooden skewer or toothpick inserted into the center comes out with just a few crumbs stuck to it. Let the cake cool for 20 minutes in the pan, then use the parchment sling to remove the cake and let it finish cooling before icing. Top the cake evenly with the cream cheese buttercream, then slice into squares and serve. Store the cake in the refrigerator, covered, for up to 2 days.

This cake is a riff on the recipe on the back of a can of Hershey's cocoa (also called Black Magic Cake), famous for including one steaming hot cup of coffee poured into the batter right before baking. I have tweaked this variation to create a tender, moist chocolate cake coated in rich ganache. It has become our favorite family celebration cake, but would also serve well as a special afternoon treat. Bittersweet Chocolate Buttercream (page 254) is also delicious on this cake.

Double Chocolate Cake

MAKES · 12 LARGE OR
24 SMALL SQUARES

1 cup [200 g] granulated sugar

1 cup [200 g] brown sugar

⅔ cup [65 g] Dutch-process cocoa powder

½ cup [112 g] vegetable or canola oil

½ cup [120 g] buttermilk, at room temperature

½ cup [120 g] sour cream, at room temperature

2 large eggs, at room temperature

2 large egg yolks, at room temperature

2 teaspoons baking soda

1 teaspoon baking powder

1 teaspoon pure vanilla extract

1 teaspoon salt

1¾ cups [250 g] all-purpose flour

¾ cup [180 g] strong, freshly brewed coffee, hot

1 recipe Ganache (page 257)

Chocolate curls, sprinkles, or chocolate pearls, for decorating

1) Position an oven rack in the middle of the oven and preheat the oven to 350°F [180°C]. Grease a 9 by 13 in [23 by 33 cm] baking pan and line with a parchment sling. 2) In a large bowl, whisk together the granulated and brown sugars, cocoa powder, oil, buttermilk, sour cream, eggs, egg yolks, baking soda, baking powder, vanilla, and salt until well combined. Add the flour and use a spatula to stir until just combined. Slowly pour the coffee into the batter and mix until just combined. 3) Pour the batter into the prepared pan. Tap the pan on the counter a few times to remove any air bubbles.

4) Bake for 28 to 35 minutes, rotating the pan halfway through, until a wooden skewer or toothpick inserted into the center comes out with the tiniest bit of crumb. Transfer the pan to a wire rack and let cool for 20 minutes. Turn the cake out onto the rack, remove the parchment paper, and let cool completely. Wrap the cake in plastic wrap and chill in the refrigerator for 30 minutes. 5) Place the chilled cake on a wire rack set over a parchment-lined sheet pan. Starting in the center of the cake, pour the ganache in a steady stream and work your way out to the edge, making sure to completely cover the surface of the cake. Continue pouring over the edges, until the sides are also completely covered. Decorate with chocolate curls, sprinkles, or chocolate pearls as desired. Let the ganache set before slicing into squares and serving. The cake can be stored in the refrigerator, covered, for up to 3 days.

CHAPTER 2

Brownies, Blondies, and Bars

"There are words
we say in the dark,
There are words we
speak in the light.
And sometimes
they're the same
words."

—Li-Young Lee

One of my previous books, *100 Cookies*, contains a recipe for my go-to brownies, which are a chewy and chocolatey reader favorite. However, over the past decade I have slowly upgraded that version by including egg yolks and more cocoa (both of which add richness) and using a bittersweet chocolate for intense flavor. Valrhona's Guanaja 70 Percent Dark Chocolate is excellent here, but your favorite chocolate will also be delectable.

Brownies 2.0

MAKES • 12 LARGE OR
24 SMALL BROWNIES

4 large eggs, at room temperature

2 large egg yolks, at room temperature

1½ cups [300 g] granulated sugar

½ cup [100 g] brown sugar

½ cup [112 g] vegetable or canola oil

2 teaspoons pure vanilla extract

¾ teaspoon salt

¾ teaspoon baking powder

8 tablespoons [1 stick or 113 g] unsalted butter

10 oz [283 g] bittersweet chocolate, chopped

⅓ cup [33 g] Dutch-process cocoa powder

1 cup plus 2 tablespoons [160 g] all-purpose flour

1) Position an oven rack in the middle of the oven and preheat the oven to 350°F [180°C]. Grease a 9 by 13 in [23 by 33 cm] baking pan and line with a parchment sling. 2) In a large bowl, whisk together the eggs, egg yolks, granulated and brown sugars, oil, vanilla, salt, and baking powder. Set aside. 3) Place the butter and chocolate in a small, heavy-bottom saucepan set over low heat and melt together, stirring frequently to prevent scorching. Continue cooking until the mixture is smooth. Remove from the heat and add the cocoa powder, whisking until completely combined. Add the chocolate mixture to the sugar-egg mixture and whisk until smooth. Add the flour and stir with a spatula until just combined. 4) Pour the batter into the prepared pan and use an offset spatula to smooth the top.

5) Bake for 22 to 27 minutes, until the sides of the brownies have set, the top is starting to crackle and look glossy, and a wooden skewer or toothpick inserted into the center comes out with crumbs. The batter on the toothpick should not be wet but should have a good amount of crumbs clinging to it. Transfer the pan to a wire rack and let cool completely. Use the parchment sling to gently lift the brownies from the pan. Cut into squares and serve. The brownies can be stored in an airtight container at room temperature for up to 2 days.

VARIATION
- **Extra-Rich Brownies:** *Bake the brownies in a 10 in [25 cm] square pan for 28 to 34 minutes.*

16

17

There was a day in my late twenties when my love for store-bought milk chocolate candy died. It was the day I was introduced to bittersweet chocolate ganache: that rich, creamy goodness now took first place in my heart. I still like milk chocolate in moderation, especially if it's paired with a darker chocolate to offset some of its sweeter notes. This brownie does just that; the milk chocolate swirl it includes is subtle but delicious.

Milk Chocolate Swirl Brownies

MAKES · 12 LARGE OR 24 SMALL BROWNIES

MILK CHOCOLATE SWIRL

3 oz [85 g] milk chocolate, finely chopped

¼ cup [60 g] heavy cream

BROWNIES

4 large eggs, at room temperature

1½ cups [300 g] granulated sugar

½ cup [100 g] brown sugar

½ cup [112 g] canola oil

2 teaspoons pure vanilla extract

1 teaspoon baking powder

¾ teaspoon salt

6 oz [170 g] semisweet or bittersweet chocolate, chopped

8 tablespoons [1 stick or 113 g] unsalted butter

¼ cup [25 g] Dutch-process cocoa powder

1½ cups [213 g] all-purpose flour

1) FOR THE MILK CHOCOLATE SWIRL Place the milk chocolate in a small heat-proof bowl. In a small saucepan over low heat, heat the heavy cream until it is simmering and just about to boil. Pour the cream over the chocolate, cover the bowl with plastic wrap, and let it sit for 5 minutes. Remove the plastic and whisk until completely smooth. Cool to room temperature. **2) FOR THE BROWNIES** Position an oven rack in the middle of the oven and preheat the oven to 350°F [180°C]. Grease a 9 by 13 in [23 by 33 cm] baking pan and line with a parchment sling. **3)** In a large bowl, whisk together the eggs, granulated and brown sugars, oil, vanilla, baking powder, and salt.

cont'd

4) Place the semisweet chocolate and butter in a small, heavy-bottom saucepan set over low heat and melt together, stirring frequently to prevent scorching. Continue cooking until the mixture is smooth. Remove from the heat and add the cocoa powder to the chocolate and whisk until completely combined. 5) Add the chocolate mixture to the sugar-egg mixture and whisk until smooth. Add the flour and stir with a spatula until just combined. 6) Pour the batter into the prepared pan and use an offset spatula to smooth the top. Dollop the milk chocolate ganache over the top and drag the tip of a butter knife through the batter, creating swirls. 7) Bake for 26 to 32 minutes, until the sides of the brownies have set, the top is starting to crackle and look glossy, and a wooden skewer or toothpick inserted into the center comes out with crumbs. The batter on the toothpick should not be wet but should have a good amount of crumbs clinging to it. 8) Transfer the pan to a wire rack and let cool completely. Use the parchment sling to gently lift the brownies from the pan. Cut into squares and serve. The brownies can be stored in an airtight container at room temperature for up to 2 days.

NOTE Leave a small space un-swirled in the center of the batter when assembling. This is the spot you want to insert your toothpick to check when the bars are done, as the swirl will remain wet throughout baking.

White chocolate in brownies will not be the hill that I die on, but if you are rolling your eyes, I will just whisper gently to you that *I've also added good old-fashioned regular chocolate here,* which I hope will entice you to try this recipe. Using a good brand of white chocolate is the key to success. I recommend Guittard's Cacao White Chocolate Baking Wafers or Valrhona Ivoire feves.

White Chocolate, Dark Chocolate Brownies

MAKES · 12 LARGE OR 24 SMALL BROWNIES

5 large eggs, at room temperature

1½ cups [300 g] granulated sugar

½ cup [100 g] brown sugar

¼ cup [56 g] vegetable or canola oil

1 tablespoon pure vanilla extract

¾ teaspoon salt

½ teaspoon baking powder

8 oz [226 g] white chocolate

8 tablespoons [1 stick or 113 g] unsalted butter

2 cups [284 g] all-purpose flour

4 oz [113 g] bittersweet chocolate, chopped into bite-size pieces

18

1) Position an oven rack in the middle of the oven and preheat the oven to 350°F [180°C]. Grease a 9 by 13 in [23 by 33 cm] baking pan and line with a parchment sling. 2) In a large bowl, whisk together the eggs, granulated and brown sugars, oil, vanilla, salt, and baking powder. 3) Place the white chocolate and butter in a small, heavy-bottom saucepan set over low heat and melt together, stirring frequently to prevent scorching. Continue cooking until the mixture is smooth.

cont'd

4) Add the white chocolate mixture to the sugar-egg mixture and whisk until smooth. Add the flour and stir with a spatula until just combined. Let the mixture cool to room temperature, then stir in the bittersweet chocolate.

5) Pour the batter into the prepared pan and use an offset spatula to smooth the top.

6) Bake the brownies for 28 to 32 minutes, until the sides of the brownies have set, the top is starting to crackle and look glossy, and a wooden skewer or toothpick inserted into the center comes out with crumbs. The batter on the toothpick should not be wet but should have a good amount of crumbs clinging to it. Transfer the pan to a wire rack and let cool completely. Use the parchment sling to gently lift the brownies from the pan. Cut them into squares and serve. The brownies can be stored in an airtight container at room temperature for up to 2 days.

NOTE Not all white chocolate is created equally. This recipe works best with a white chocolate that has at least 30 percent cocoa butter. These brownies can be made with a store-brand baking white chocolate bar, but please note that the papery top on the brownies will separate more as it bakes with lower percentage cocoa butter chocolate and will seem hard out of the oven. They will still taste good, and the top will soften as they cool.

Bananas and chocolate are a personal favorite, and combining my best banana bread recipe with my favorite brownie recipe might have been a stroke of genius. Or, just the opposite: This is so obvious, why didn't I do this years ago? These bars take a little longer to put together since there are two separate bases, but I promise it's worth your time.

Banana Bread Brownies

MAKES · 12 LARGE OR
24 SMALL BROWNIES

BROWNIE BASE

2 large eggs, at room temperature

¾ cup [150 g] granulated sugar

¼ cup [50 g] brown sugar

¼ cup [56 g] vegetable or canola oil

1 teaspoon pure vanilla extract

½ teaspoon salt

½ teaspoon baking powder

4 oz [113 g] semisweet or bittersweet chocolate, finely chopped

4 tablespoons [56 g] unsalted butter

2 tablespoons Dutch-process cocoa powder

¾ cup [107 g] all-purpose flour

BANANA BREAD

½ cup [113 g] mashed very ripe bananas

¼ cup [50 g] granulated sugar

¼ cup [50 g] brown sugar

¼ cup [60 g] buttermilk, at room temperature

1 large egg, at room temperature

3 tablespoons unsalted butter, melted and cooled

2 tablespoons vegetable or canola oil

1 teaspoon pure vanilla extract

½ teaspoon baking soda

½ teaspoon salt

¾ cup [107 g] all-purpose flour

1) Position an oven rack in the middle of the oven and preheat the oven to 350°F [180°C]. Grease a 9 in [23 cm] square baking pan and line with a parchment sling. 2) FOR THE BROWNIE BASE In a large bowl, whisk together the eggs, granulated and brown sugars, oil, vanilla, salt, and baking powder. 3) Place the chocolate and butter in a small, heavy-bottom saucepan set over low heat and melt together, stirring frequently to prevent scorching. Continue cooking until the mixture is smooth. Remove from the heat and add the cocoa powder to the chocolate and whisk until completely combined. 4) Add the chocolate mixture to the sugar-egg mixture and whisk until smooth. Add the flour and stir with a spatula until just combined. 5) FOR THE BANANA BREAD In a large bowl, whisk together the bananas, granulated and brown sugars, buttermilk, egg, melted butter, oil, vanilla, baking soda, and salt. Add the flour and stir with a spatula until just combined.

19

6) **TO ASSEMBLE** Pour three-quarters of the brownie batter into the pan and smooth the top. Spread the banana batter over the brownie batter, then dollop the remaining brownie batter over the top. Drag the tip of a butter knife through the batter, making a figure-eight motion to create swirls and semi-combine the batter. You want the batters to mingle, but there should also be distinct swirls of each one. 7) Bake for 30 to 38 minutes, until a wooden skewer or toothpick inserted into the brownies comes out with crumbs. The brownie batter on the toothpick should not be wet but should have a good amount of crumbs clinging to it. Transfer the pan to a wire rack and let cool completely. Use the parchment sling to gently lift the brownies from the pan. Cut them into bars and serve. The brownies can be stored in an airtight container at room temperature for up to 2 days.

One of the most-made recipes in *100 Cookies* is the Cinnamon Roll Blondies, and over the years, I've come up with several variations on these beloved bars. Banana was a perfect addition: The blondies are rich and nutty, with good banana bread flavor and a tangy swirl of cream cheese.

MAKES · 9 LARGE
OR 12 SMALL
BLONDIES

Brown Butter Banana Blondies

20

CREAM CHEESE SWIRL

3 oz [85 g] cream cheese, at room temperature

3 tablespoons granulated sugar

BLONDIES

12 tablespoons [1½ sticks or 170 g] unsalted butter

1½ cups [300 g] brown sugar

½ cup [113 g] mashed very ripe bananas

1 tablespoon pure vanilla extract

¾ teaspoon salt

1 large egg, at room temperature

1½ teaspoons baking powder

1½ cups [213 g] all-purpose flour

1) Position an oven rack in the middle of the oven and preheat the oven to 350°F [180°C]. Grease an 8 in [20 cm] square baking pan and line with a parchment sling. 2) FOR THE CREAM CHEESE SWIRL In a medium bowl, combine the cream cheese and granulated sugar with a spatula until smooth and completely combined. 3) FOR THE BLONDIES In a large saucepan over medium-high heat, brown the butter until it is dark golden brown and is giving off a nutty aroma, 2 to 3 minutes (for tips on browning butter, see page 276). Remove from the heat and add the brown sugar, banana, vanilla, and salt. Add the egg and baking powder and whisk until combined. Add the flour and stir with a spatula until just combined.

4) Transfer the batter to the prepared pan and pat into an even layer. Dollop the cream cheese mixture over the top of the batter. Drag the tip of a butter knife through the batter, creating swirls. 5) Bake for 22 to 28 minutes, until the blondies are set on the edges, the top is golden brown and beginning to form cracks, and a wooden skewer or toothpick inserted into the blondies comes out slightly wet with just a couple of crumbs. Transfer the pan to a wire rack and let cool completely. Use the parchment sling to gently lift the blondies from the pan. Cut into squares and serve. The blondies can be stored in an airtight container at room temperature for up to 2 days.

NOTE Leave a small space unswirled in the center of the batter when assembling. This is the spot you want to insert your toothpick to check when the bars are done, as the cream cheese swirl will remain wet throughout baking.

There's a lot of trash talk about blondies, mostly because they are not brownies, but also because they can be compared to cake or described as "cakey." As a lifelong blondie fan, I can't get on board with this slander. So I will give you this important key to getting a blondie right: Underbake it slightly. Please. An overbaked blondie is cakey and boring, and not gooey, rich, and fabulous as it is meant to be. I make these blondies in an 8 in [20 cm] square pan so they are extra thick and rich.

Bourbon Blondies

MAKES · 9 LARGE OR
12 SMALL BLONDIES

12 tablespoons [1½ sticks or 170 g] unsalted butter

1½ cups [300 g] dark brown sugar

¾ teaspoon salt

2 tablespoons bourbon

1 tablespoon pure vanilla extract

1 large egg, at room temperature

1½ teaspoons baking powder

1½ cups [213 g] all-purpose flour

3 oz [85 g] semisweet or bittersweet chocolate, chopped

Flaky salt, for sprinkling (optional)

21

1) Position an oven rack in the middle of the oven and preheat the oven to 350°F [180°C]. Grease an 8 in [20 cm] square baking pan and line with a parchment sling. 2) In a large saucepan over medium heat, melt the butter, brown sugar, and salt. Remove from the heat and stir in the bourbon and vanilla. Let the mixture cool to room temperature. Add the egg and baking powder and whisk until combined. Add the flour and stir with a spatula until just combined. Add the chocolate and stir gently. 3) Transfer the batter to the prepared pan and pat into an even layer. Sprinkle the top with flaky salt (if using).

4) Bake for 22 to 26 minutes, until the blondies are set on the edges, the top is golden brown and beginning to form cracks, and a wooden skewer or toothpick inserted into the blondies comes out slightly wet with just a couple of crumbs. Transfer the pan to a wire rack and let cool completely. Use the parchment sling to gently lift the blondies from the pan. Cut into squares and serve. The blondies can be stored in an airtight container at room temperature for up to 2 days.

I'm not sure how these blondies evolved—I only know that my family is addicted to them, and I fear you will be too. They combine the perfect crunch and peanut butter flavor of a Scotcharoo bar with the gooey, brown-sugary goodness of a blondie. Each bite leads to another, and there is no escape once you've made them.

MAKES · 12 LARGE OR
24 SMALL BLONDIES

Scotcharoo Blondies

PEANUT BUTTER CRUNCH

½ cup [108 g] creamy peanut butter

3 tablespoons corn syrup

2 tablespoons unsalted butter

¾ cup [135 g] butterscotch chips

4 cups [120 g] Rice Krispies cereal

BLONDIES

12 tablespoons [1½ sticks or 170 g] unsalted butter

1½ cups [300 g] brown sugar

¾ teaspoon salt

4 teaspoons pure vanilla extract

1 large egg, at room temperature

1½ teaspoons baking powder

1½ cups [213 g] all-purpose flour

½ cup [85 g] semisweet or bittersweet chocolate, chopped

1) Position an oven rack in the middle of the oven and preheat the oven to 350°F [180°C]. Grease a 9 by 13 in [23 by 33 cm] baking pan and line with a parchment sling.

2) **FOR THE PEANUT BUTTER CRUNCH** In a large, heavy-bottom saucepan over medium heat, melt the peanut butter, corn syrup, and butter. Add the butterscotch chips and stir until smooth (this will take a few minutes). Remove from the heat and pour the cereal into the hot mixture and use a spatula to stir until completely combined.

3) Pour the mixture into the prepared pan and press it down into the pan in a compact layer, making sure the top is smooth. Set aside while you make the blondie batter.

4) FOR THE BLONDIES In a medium sauce-pan over medium heat, melt the butter, brown sugar, and salt. Remove from the heat and stir in the vanilla. Let the mixture cool to room temperature. Add the egg and baking powder and whisk to combine. Add the flour and use a spatula to stir until just combined. Add the chopped chocolate and stir again until the chocolate is evenly distributed. Pour the batter over the peanut butter crunch layer and use an offset spatula to spread it evenly over the top. The batter will be very thick and it will seem like just a thin layer across the top, but it will puff up nicely in the oven. **5)** Bake for 22 to 26 minutes, until the blondies are set on the edges, the top is golden brown and just beginning to form cracks, and a wooden skewer or toothpick inserted into the center comes out with just a couple of crumbs. Transfer the pan to a wire rack and let cool completely. Use the parchment sling to gently lift the blondies from the pan. Cut into squares and serve. The blondies can be stored in an airtight container for up to 2 days.

22

23

I am a huge fan of toasted sesame oil and use it often in my baking, especially in cookies. It pairs beautifully with brown sugar, so putting it in blondies seemed only natural. These blondies bake up thick and gooey with lots of sesame flavor. I like a whole tablespoon of toasted sesame oil, but you can start with just a teaspoon if desired.

Toasted Sesame Blondies

MAKES · 9 LARGE OR
12 SMALL BLONDIES

12 tablespoons [1½ sticks or 170 g] unsalted butter

1½ cups [300 g] dark brown sugar

¾ teaspoon salt

1 tablespoon toasted sesame oil

1 tablespoon pure vanilla extract

1 large egg, at room temperature

1½ teaspoons baking powder

1½ cups [213 g] all-purpose flour

3 tablespoons black or white sesame seeds, or a combination, for sprinkling

1) Position an oven rack in the middle of the oven and preheat the oven to 350°F [180°C]. Grease an 8 in [20 cm] square baking pan and line with a parchment sling. 2) In a medium saucepan over medium heat, melt the butter, brown sugar, and salt. Remove from the heat and stir in the toasted sesame oil and vanilla. Let the mixture cool to room temperature. Add the egg and baking powder and whisk until combined. Add the flour and use a spatula to stir until just combined. 3) Transfer the batter to the prepared pan and use the back of a spoon or an offset spatula to smooth the top. Sprinkle the top evenly with the sesame seeds. 4) Bake for 24 to 28 minutes, until the blondies are set on the edges, the top is golden brown and just beginning to form cracks, and a wooden skewer or toothpick inserted into the blondies comes out with just a couple of crumbs. Transfer the pan to a wire rack and let cool completely. Use the parchment sling to gently lift the blondies from the pan. Cut them into bars and serve. The blondies can be stored in an airtight container for up to 2 days.

Every winter holiday of my childhood had a sugar cookie decorating day. There were years when it was just my mom, my sister, and me sprinkling cookie tops with red and green. At some point my little brother came along and enjoyed dumping bottles of sprinkles over a single cookie. Sometimes a family friend would join in for a few hours, laughing with my mom or helping break up fights between me and my sister. My grandma would usually make an appearance, sipping coffee at the kitchen table and shaking her head at our mini disasters. Sugar cookie bars aren't quite as creative as those individual cookies, but they are just as delicious and involve less fighting. Frosting and sprinkles can be added on top if desired.

MAKES · 12 LARGE
OR 24 SMALL BARS

Sugar Cookie Bars

2½ cups [355 g] all-purpose flour

1 teaspoon baking powder

½ teaspoon baking soda

½ teaspoon cream of tartar

12 tablespoons [1½ sticks or 170 g] unsalted butter, at room temperature

1½ cups [300 g] granulated sugar, plus more for sprinkling

¾ teaspoon salt

2 large eggs, at room temperature

1 large egg yolk, at room temperature

1 tablespoon pure vanilla extract

1) Position an oven rack in the middle of the oven and preheat the oven to 350°F [180°C]. Grease a 9 by 13 in [23 by 33 cm] baking pan and line with a parchment sling. 2) In a medium bowl, combine the flour, baking powder, baking soda, and cream of tartar. 3) In the bowl of a stand mixer fitted with a paddle, beat the butter on medium speed until creamy, about 1 minute. Add the granulated sugar and salt and beat on medium speed until light and fluffy, 2 to 3 minutes. Add the eggs, egg yolk, and vanilla and beat on medium speed until combined. Add the flour mixture and beat on low speed until just combined.

4) Transfer the dough to the prepared pan and use your hands to smooth it into an even layer. Sprinkle the top generously and evenly with coarse sugar. 5) For soft, chewy bars, bake for 24 to 28 minutes, until light golden brown and a wooden skewer or toothpick inserted into the center comes out clean. For bars with crisp tops and bottoms, bake for 28 to 32 minutes, until the bars are golden brown. Transfer the pan to a wire rack and let cool completely. Use the parchment sling to gently lift the bars from the pan. Cut into squares and serve. The bars can be stored in an airtight container in the refrigerator for up to 3 days.

24

VARIATION

• **Sugar Cookie Bars with Frosting (pictured):** *Omit topping the bars with sugar. Use a single recipe of the Cream Cheese Buttercream (page 250) to top the cooled bars. Before the icing sets, cover with sprinkles, if desired.*

I've always been enamored with iced oatmeal cookies, but they are often disappointing and overly sweet. I found soaking the raisins in rum helped, along with a little orange zest, cinnamon, and nutmeg. More rum in the icing helped too. This is one tasty pan of bars to spend the afternoon with.

Raisin Rum Bars

MAKES · 12 LARGE OR
24 SMALL BARS

BARS

¾ cup [105 g] raisins

⅓ cup [80 g] dark rum

2 cups [180 g] rolled oats

1½ cups [213 g]
all-purpose flour

¾ teaspoon baking soda

¾ teaspoon ground
cinnamon

¼ teaspoon freshly
grated nutmeg

12 tablespoons [1½ sticks
or 170 g] unsalted butter,
at room temperature

¾ cup [150 g]
granulated sugar

¾ cup [150 g]
brown sugar

1 tablespoon orange zest

¾ teaspoon salt

1 large egg, at room
temperature

2 teaspoons
pure vanilla extract

ICING

2 tablespoons unsalted
butter, melted

2 to 4 tablespoons
reserved rum or water

Pinch of salt

2 cups [240 g]
confectioners' sugar

1) FOR THE BARS In a small bowl, combine the raisins and rum. Let the raisins soak for 20 minutes. Strain the raisins and reserve the rum. 2) Position an oven rack in the middle of the oven and preheat the oven to 350°F [180°C]. Grease a 9 by 13 in [23 by 33 cm] baking pan and line with a parchment sling. 3) In a medium bowl, combine the oats, flour, baking soda, cinnamon, and nutmeg. 4) In the bowl of a stand mixer fitted with a paddle, beat the butter on medium speed until creamy, about 1 minute. Add the granulated and brown sugars, orange zest, and salt and beat on medium speed until light and fluffy, 2 to 3 minutes. Add the egg and vanilla and mix on medium speed until combined. Add the flour mixture and mix on low speed until just combined, then add the soaked raisins and

finish mixing on low speed. Using a spatula, stir the batter to incorporate any stray oats from the bottom of the mixing bowl. 5) Transfer the dough to the prepared pan and pat into an even layer. 6) Bake for 20 to 26 minutes, until the top is light golden brown and a wooden skewer or toothpick inserted into the center comes out clean.

7) FOR THE ICING While the bars are baking, in a medium bowl, whisk together the butter, 2 tablespoons of reserved rum, and salt. Add the confectioners' sugar and whisk until well combined and smooth. Add more rum if necessary, 1 tablespoon at a time, until the icing is thick but pourable. 8) Transfer the baking pan to a wire rack and immediately pour the icing over the warm bars, using an offset spatula to smooth it over the top. Let the bars cool to room temperature, then cut into squares and serve. The bars can be stored in an airtight container for up to 3 days.

25

What every hot summer day needs is creamy, berry-filled bars.
I find adding a tablespoon (or two) of raspberry vodka to
the filling adds a nice punch of raspberry flavor.

MAKES · 12 LARGE OR
24 SMALL BARS

Creamy Raspberry Bars

RASPBERRY FILLING

1 lb [455 g] fresh
raspberries

¼ cup [50 g] granulated
sugar

2 tablespoons water

Two 14 oz [396 g] cans
sweetened condensed
milk

¼ cup [16 g] freeze-
dried raspberry powder
(see page 16)

3 tablespoons heavy
cream

2 tablespoons raspberry
vodka (optional)

1 teaspoon lemon juice

1 teaspoon pure vanilla
extract

¼ teaspoon salt

CRUST

2 cups [284 g]
all-purpose flour

1½ cups [150 g] almond
flour or rolled oats

½ cup [100 g] brown
sugar

¼ cup [50 g] granulated
sugar

2 tablespoons cacao nibs

½ teaspoon baking soda

½ teaspoon salt

1 cup [2 sticks or 227 g]
unsalted butter, at room
temperature

1) Position an oven rack in the middle of
the oven and preheat the oven to 350°F
[180°C]. Grease a 9 by 13 in [23 by 33 cm]
baking pan and line with a parchment
sling. 2) FOR THE RASPBERRY FILLING In
a medium saucepan over medium heat,
combine the fresh berries, granulated
sugar, and water. Cook for 10 to 12 minutes,
until the berries have broken down and
released their juices. Strain the berries over
a large bowl through a fine-mesh sieve,
pressing on the berries to release all their
liquid. Discard the berries. 3) In the large
bowl, whisk together the cooked berry juice,
sweetened condensed milk, freeze-dried
berry powder, heavy cream, raspberry
vodka (if using), lemon juice, vanilla, and
salt. 4) FOR THE CRUST In the bowl of a
stand mixer fitted with a paddle, combine
the all-purpose flour, almond flour, brown

and granulated sugars, cacao nibs, baking soda, and salt and mix on low speed to combine. Add the butter and mix on medium speed until the mixture is crumbly. 5) TO ASSEMBLE Press half of the crust mixture into the bottom of the prepared pan. Bake for 10 minutes. Remove the pan from the oven and carefully spread the filling over the crust, then sprinkle the remaining crust mixture evenly over the top.

Bake for 15 to 20 minutes, until the filling is set and does not jiggle, and the crumbly top is light golden brown. 6) Transfer the pan to a wire rack and let cool to room temperature. Place the pan in the refrigerator and chill for 4 to 6 hours. Slice the bars into squares and serve. The bars can be served cold or at room temperature and keep best in an airtight container in the refrigerator for up to 3 days.

"There among the trees, / the yellow of the lemons is revealed; / and the chill in the heart / thaws, and deep in us / the golden horns of sunlight / pelt their songs," Eugenio Montale observes in his poem "The Lemons," and I wonder if it is trite to apply his words to lemon bars. But I can't deny that on chilly winter afternoons, a burst of lemon glaze and a bite of lemon cake has this same effect on my soul.

Lemon Cake Squares

MAKES · 12 LARGE OR
24 SMALL SQUARES

CAKE SQUARES
1¾ cups [250 g]
all-purpose flour

½ teaspoon baking soda

14 tablespoons [196 g]
unsalted butter, at room
temperature

1½ cups [300 g]
granulated sugar

1 tablespoon lemon zest

½ teaspoon salt

3 large eggs, at room
temperature

2 large egg yolks, at
room temperature

2 tablespoons sour
cream

1 teaspoon pure vanilla
extract

⅓ cup [80 g] lemon juice

LEMON GLAZE
2 tablespoons unsalted
butter, melted

Pinch of salt

2 to 4 tablespoons lemon
juice

2 cups [240 g]
confectioners' sugar

1) FOR THE CAKE SQUARES Position an oven rack in the middle of the oven and preheat the oven to 350°F [180°C]. Grease a 9 by 13 in [23 by 33 cm] baking pan and line with a parchment sling. 2) In a medium bowl, whisk together the flour and baking soda. 3) In the bowl of a stand mixer fitted with a paddle, beat the butter on medium speed until creamy, about 1 minute. Add the granulated sugar, lemon zest, and salt and beat on medium speed until very light and fluffy, 4 to 6 minutes. Scrape down the sides of the bowl and add the eggs one at a time, beating on medium speed until incorporated and stopping to scrape down the sides of the bowl after each addition. Add the egg yolks, sour cream, and vanilla and mix on low speed to combine. Add half of the flour mixture and mix on low speed until combined. Add the lemon juice and mix on low speed until combined. Add the

remaining flour mixture and mix on low speed until combined. Increase the speed to medium and beat for 15 to 20 seconds. 4) Pour the batter into the prepared pan and use an offset spatula to smooth the top. 5) Bake for 22 to 28 minutes, rotating the pan halfway through, until a wooden skewer or toothpick inserted near the center comes out clean. 6) **FOR THE LEMON GLAZE** Meanwhile, make the glaze: In a medium bowl, whisk together the melted butter, salt, and 1 tablespoon of lemon juice until combined. Add the confectioners' sugar and mix again until smooth. Add more lemon juice, 1 tablespoon at a time, to thin the glaze to your preferred consistency. The glaze should be thick but pourable. 7) Transfer the baking pan to a wire rack. Pour the glaze evenly over the warm cake and let set. Remove the cake from the pan using the parchment sling. Cut into squares and serve. Alternatively, the cake can be left in the pan and covered in plastic wrap, then stored in the refrigerator for up to 2 days.

27

These cookie bars are based on breakfast cookies from *100 Morning Treats*, which are a riff on the rye-cranberry chocolate chunk cookies from Dorie Greenspan's excellent book *Baking with Dorie*. While I like both versions equally, baking them in a pan and then cutting them into squares saves a lot of time, and makes for a perfect after-school (or after-work) snack.

Chocolate Rye Cookie Bars

MAKES · 12 LARGE OR 24 SMALL BARS

1½ cups [213 g] all-purpose flour

1 cup [130 g] rye flour

¾ cup [68 g] old-fashioned rolled oats

¼ cup [36 g] whole-wheat flour

3 tablespoons white sesame seeds, plus more for sprinkling

2 tablespoons flaxseed

2 teaspoons baking powder

1 teaspoon baking soda

1 cup [2 sticks or 227 g] unsalted butter, at room temperature

1 cup [200 g] granulated sugar

1 cup [200 g] brown sugar

1 teaspoon salt

2 large eggs, at room temperature

1 tablespoon pure vanilla extract

4 oz [113 g] semisweet chocolate, coarsely chopped

½ cup [70 g] King Arthur Orange Jammy Bits or dried cherries, chopped

½ cup [60 g] toasted pecans, chopped into bite-size pieces

⅓ cup [45 g] poppy seeds

28

1) Position an oven rack in the middle of the oven and preheat the oven to 350°F [180°C]. Grease a 9 by 13 in [23 by 33 cm] pan or a 10 in [25 cm] square pan and line with a parchment sling. 2) In the bowl of a food processor, process the all-purpose flour, rye flour, rolled oats, whole-wheat flour, white sesame seeds, flaxseed, baking powder, and baking soda until the rolled oats are broken down, about ten pulses. 3) In the bowl of a stand mixer fitted with a paddle, beat the butter on medium speed until creamy, about 1 minute. Add the granulated and brown sugars and salt and continue beating until light and fluffy, 3 to 5 minutes. Add the eggs and vanilla, beating until incorporated, stopping to scrape down the sides of the bowl

as needed. Add the flour mixture on low speed, beating until incorporated. Add the chocolate, orange bits, pecans, and poppy seeds and mix until completely incorporated. 4) Transfer the dough to the prepared pan and pat into an even layer. Sprinkle with white sesame seeds. 5) Bake for 26 to 32 minutes, until the bars are golden and a wooden skewer or toothpick inserted into the center comes out with the slightest bit of crumb. Transfer the pan to a wire rack and let cool completely. Use the parchment sling to gently lift the bars from the pan. Cut into squares and serve. The bars can be stored in an airtight container at room temperature for up to 2 days.

Throughout my childhood, baked meringue was always a disappointment to me—I wanted cool, creamy whipped cream on those pies and bars, not overly sweet egg whites. My grandma did not share this opinion, however, and topped many of her pies with a thick layer. Now that I'm older, I've grown to appreciate meringue, even in baked form. I prefer it swirled into batter, as both the meringue and the batter benefit from intermingling; the batter is lightened slightly, and the sweetness of the meringue is tempered by the flavors in the batter.

Chocolate Meringue Bars

MAKES · 12 LARGE OR 24 SMALL BARS

BARS

12 tablespoons [1½ sticks or 170 g] unsalted butter

1½ cups [300 g] brown sugar

¾ teaspoon salt

⅓ cup [33 g] Dutch-process cocoa powder

1 tablespoon pure vanilla extract

1 large egg, at room temperature

1½ teaspoons baking powder

1½ cups [213 g] all-purpose flour

ASSEMBLY

1 recipe Meringue (page 258), brown sugar variation

1 tablespoon finely ground espresso

⅓ cup [40 g] cacao nibs, finely chopped

1) FOR THE BARS Position an oven rack in the middle of the oven and preheat the oven to 350°F [180°C]. Grease a 9 by 13 in [23 by 33 cm] baking pan and line with a parchment sling. **2)** In a medium saucepan over medium heat, melt the butter, brown sugar, and salt. Remove from the heat and stir in the cocoa powder and vanilla. Let the mixture cool to room temperature. Add the egg and baking powder and whisk to combine. Add the flour and stir with a spatula until just combined. **3)** Transfer the batter to the prepared pan and pat into an even layer. **4)** FOR ASSEMBLY Make the meringue as directed, mixing in the ground espresso along with the vanilla, then stirring

29

in the cacao nibs to combine. 5) Working quickly, spoon the meringue over the chocolate batter and fold it into the batter gently with a butter knife six or seven times using a figure-eight motion, then smooth the top. There should still be a visible amount of meringue on the top, which will bake up as a topping. 6) Bake for 36 to 45 minutes, until the top of the meringue is browned and a wooden skewer or toothpick inserted into the center of the bars comes out clean (make sure to check the cake portion of the bars and not just the meringue). Transfer the pan to a wire rack to cool. Once cooled, remove the bars from the pan using the parchment sling and slice into squares. The bars can be stored in an airtight container at room temperature for up to 2 days.

When I first started baking, I found making pie bars to be less intimidating than making an actual pie, with results equally delicious and less time consuming. For this recipe, I streamlined a typical pecan pie by using a pat-in-the-pan crust for ease, sweetened condensed milk for rich flavor, and espresso to help cut some of the sweetness. There is also chocolate involved.

MAKES · 12 LARGE
OR 24 SMALL BARS

Pecan Espresso Bars

CRUST

1 recipe Pat-in-the-Pan-
Pie Dough (page 262),
pecan variation

FILLING

One 14 oz [396 g]
can sweetened
condensed milk

1 large egg, at room
temperature

1 tablespoon pure vanilla
extract

1 tablespoon Kahlúa

2 teaspoons finely
ground espresso or
coffee beans

¼ teaspoon salt

1 cup [170 g] semisweet
chocolate chips

1½ cups [180 g] pecans
toasted and chopped
into bite-size pieces

2 oz [57] bittersweet
chocolate, chopped into
bite-size pieces

30

1) FOR THE CRUST Position an oven rack in the middle of the oven and preheat the oven to 350°F [180°C]. Grease an 8 in [20 cm] square baking pan and line with a parchment sling. 2) Transfer the dough into the prepared pan, smoothing it with your hands to an even thickness. 3) Bake the crust for 20 minutes, until the dough is no longer wet to the touch. 4) FOR THE FILLING While the crust bakes, in a medium bowl, whisk together the sweetened condensed milk, egg, vanilla, Kahlúa, ground espresso, and salt. 5) Remove the baking pan from the oven and scatter the semisweet chocolate chips over the top of the crust (be careful, the pan is hot!). Return to the oven for 2 minutes, then remove again and use the back of a spoon to spread the chocolate into an even layer. Scatter 1 cup [120 g] of the pecans over the chocolate.

6) Pour the filling evenly over the crust, then top with the remaining ½ cup [60 g] of pecans and the bittersweet chocolate. 7) Return the pan to the oven and bake for 24 to 30 minutes, until the filling barely jiggles in the center when the pan is shaken (if the filling makes a waving motion when you shake the pan, the bars need more time). 8) Transfer the pan to a wire rack to cool. After 5 minutes, run a knife around the edges of the bars (if the sweetened condensed milk gets between the parchment lining and the pan at all, the bars will stick and can be hard to remove from the pan). Refrigerate the bars for 2 hours or covered overnight, then slice into squares and serve. The bars can be stored in an airtight container in the refrigerator for up to 3 days.

31

I first encountered chocolate chip cookie bars at church-ordained potlucks; many, many families brought them. As a child, I avoided all the questionable casseroles lining the tables and skipped straight to the desserts, so I was very familiar with these bars and all their variations. Most of them were based on the iconic Nestlé Toll House recipe, and I made sure to look for bars that were golden yet soft, with chocolate chips dotted in the batter in a healthy ratio, and absolutely no walnuts. I've tried to re-create similar bars here, and I started with my own cookie base, tinkering until I got them just right.

Chocolate Chip Bars

MAKES · 12 LARGE OR
24 SMALL BARS

2½ cups [355 g] all-purpose flour

1 teaspoon baking powder

½ teaspoon baking soda

1 cup [2 sticks or 227 g] unsalted butter, at room temperature

1 cup [200 g] brown sugar

¾ cup [150 g] granulated sugar

1 teaspoon salt

2 large eggs, at room temperature

1 tablespoon pure vanilla extract

1½ cups [256 g] semisweet chocolate chips

1) Position an oven rack in the middle of the oven and preheat the oven to 350°F [180°C]. Grease a 9 by 13 in [23 by 33 cm] baking pan and line with a parchment sling. 2) In a medium bowl, whisk together the flour, baking powder, and baking soda. 3) In the bowl of a stand mixer fitted with a paddle, beat the butter on medium speed until creamy, about 1 minute. Add the brown and granulated sugars and salt and beat on medium speed until light and fluffy, 2 to 3 minutes. Scrape down the sides of the bowl, add the eggs and vanilla, and mix until smooth. Add the flour mixture and beat on low speed until just combined. Add the chocolate chips and mix on low speed. 4) Transfer the dough to the prepared pan and use an offset spatula to spread it evenly, or lightly grease a piece of plastic with nonstick cooking spray and use it to press the dough into the pan in an even layer. 5) Bake for 24 to 30 minutes, until the bars are golden brown and a wooden skewer or toothpick inserted into the bars comes out with the tiniest bit of crumb. 6) Transfer the pan to a wire rack and let cool completely. Use the parchment sling to gently lift the bars from the pan. Cut into squares and serve. The bars can be stored in an airtight container at room temperature for up to 2 days.

VARIATION

• **M&M's Bars:** *Replace the 1½ cups [256 g] of semisweet chocolate chips with 6 oz [170 g] of chopped M&M's.*

This is a recipe I made at several coffeehouse bakeries I worked at—customers couldn't say no to the chocolate fudge center and oat crust, convincing themselves that the marriage of decadent filling to a "healthy" base was an acceptable reason to eat one every afternoon. I didn't question their intuition. I've updated the recipe a bit throughout the years by adding more salt and cocoa powder for a more intense flavor.

Oatmeal Fudge Bars

MAKES · 12 LARGE
OR 24 SMALL BARS

CRUST

2½ cups [250 g] rolled or quick oats

¾ cup [107 g] all-purpose flour

¾ cup [150 g] brown sugar

½ teaspoon baking soda

½ teaspoon salt

12 tablespoons [1½ sticks or 170 g] unsalted butter, cut into 1 in [2.5 cm] pieces, at room temperature

FILLING

12 tablespoons [1½ sticks or 170 g] unsalted butter

4 oz [113 g] semisweet chocolate chips

1 tablespoon Dutch-process cocoa powder

1 cup [200 g] granulated sugar

1 cup [200 g] brown sugar

1 teaspoon salt

1 teaspoon pure vanilla

4 large eggs, at room temperature

1 teaspoon baking powder

1¼ cups [178 g] all-purpose flour

32

1) Position an oven rack in the middle of the oven and preheat the oven to 350°F [180°C]. Grease a 9 by 13 in [23 by 33 cm] baking pan and line with a parchment sling. 2) FOR THE CRUST In the bowl of a stand mixer fitted with a paddle, combine the oats, flour, brown sugar, baking soda, and salt. Add the butter, one piece at a time, beating until the mixture resembles coarse sand. Remove 1 cup [125 g] of the mixture and set it aside in a small bowl. Press the rest of the mixture into the bottom of the prepared pan. 3) FOR THE FILLING Place the butter and chocolate chips in a large, heavy-bottom saucepan set over low heat and melt together, stirring frequently to prevent scorching. Continue cooking until the mixture is smooth. Remove from the heat and add the cocoa powder and whisk until combined. Add the granulated and brown sugars, salt, and vanilla and whisk again. Let the mixture cool to room temperature. Add the eggs and baking powder and whisk until smooth. Add the flour and stir with a spatula until just combined. 4) Pour the filling over the crust, then sprinkle the reserved crust mixture over the chocolate filling. It won't completely cover it, but that's okay. 5) Bake for 22 to 28 minutes, until the filling is set and the topping is golden brown. Transfer the pan to a wire rack and let cool. Cut the bars into squares and serve. The bars can be kept in an airtight container for up to 3 days.

CHAPTER 3

Pie Bakes

"Pies are just sweet calzones, honey, and I'm good at making calzones."

—Ben Wyatt, *Parks and Recreation*

33

Chocolate + shortbread + caramel = a perfect trio. This is my favorite way to combine the three, sometimes known as a "millionaire" dessert. I add a little splash of triple sec because the faint hit of orange adds brightness. Flaky salt on top can be a pretty final touch.

Millionaire Pie

MAKES · ONE 10 IN [25 CM] TART

CRUST

10 tablespoons [140 g] unsalted butter, at room temperature

⅓ cup [65 g] granulated sugar

½ teaspoon salt

2 large egg yolks

1 teaspoon pure vanilla extract

2 cups [284 g] all-purpose flour

Egg wash (see page 16)

CARAMEL

2 cups [400 g] granulated sugar

¼ cup [80 g] corn syrup

2 tablespoons water

¼ teaspoon salt

2 cups [480 g] heavy cream

¼ cup [60 g] Crème Fraîche (page 278)

14 tablespoons [196 g] unsalted butter, cut into 1 in [2.5 cm] pieces

1 tablespoon triple sec or other orange liqueur

1 tablespoon pure vanilla extract

1 recipe Ganache (page 257)

1) FOR THE CRUST In the bowl of a stand mixer fitted with a paddle, beat the butter on medium speed until creamy, about 1 minute. Add the granulated sugar and salt and mix on medium speed until light and creamy, 2 to 3 minutes. Add the egg yolks and vanilla and mix on low speed until combined. Add the flour and mix on low speed until combined. 2) Press the mixture into the bottom and up the sides of a 10 in [23 cm] tart pan with a removeable bottom (see note, page 106). Press and smooth the dough with your hands to an even thickness. 3) Transfer the pan to the freezer until the dough is firm, 20 to 30 minutes.

cont'd

4) Position an oven rack in the middle of the oven and preheat the oven to 350°F [180°C]. Remove the pan from the freezer and line the crust with parchment paper, covering the edges to prevent burning. Fill the center with pie weights. 5) Bake for 22 to 28 minutes, until the dough is light golden brown and no longer wet. Remove the tart pan from the oven and carefully remove the pie weights and parchment paper. Brush the center of the tart with the egg wash. Return the pan to the oven and bake for 3 to 6 more minutes, until deep golden brown. Transfer the pan to a wire rack and let cool completely. 6) FOR THE CARAMEL In a large, heavy-bottom saucepan, combine the granulated sugar, corn syrup, water, and salt, stirring very gently to combine while trying to avoid getting any sugar crystals on the sides of the pan. Cover the pan and bring to a boil over medium-high heat until the sugar has melted and the mixture is clear, 3 to 5 minutes. Uncover and cook until the sugar has turned a pale golden color and registers 300°F [150°C] on an instant-read thermometer, 4 to 5 minutes. Turn the heat down slightly and cook for a few minutes more until the sugar is golden and registers 350°F [180°C]. Immediately remove the pan from the heat and carefully add about ½ cup [120 g] of the heavy cream. (The cream will foam considerably and may seize, but this is normal.) Continue to add the heavy cream, a little bit at a time, until it is all incorporated. Add the crème fraîche. Add the butter, one piece at a time, stirring after each addition, followed by the triple sec and vanilla, and stir to combine. Set the pan back over medium heat and cook, stirring constantly, until any

hard pieces have melted. Increase the heat to medium-high and cook, stirring frequently, until the caramel registers 240°F [115°C] (this is the soft-ball stage), 8 to 10 minutes. Remove from the heat and set aside to cool for 5 to 10 minutes. Pour the warm caramel into the baked, cooled crust and let set at room temperature, about 2 hours. 7) TO ASSEMBLE Starting in the center of the pan, pour the warm ganache over the caramel in a steady stream and work your way out to the edge, making sure to completely cover the surface of the caramel. Refrigerate until set, about 1 hour. When ready to serve, let the tart sit at room temperature for 1 hour, then slice and serve. The tart can be stored in the refrigerator, covered, for up to 2 days.

NOTE Tart pans come in many different depths; some are very shallow. You will need a pan that has at least 1½ in [4 cm] sides for this recipe.

I went through a chocolate peanut butter pie phase in high school. Our local Baker's Square Pie Shoppe served one, and it was pure indulgence: a flaky base filled with a chocolate–peanut butter mixture and topped with whipped cream and peanut butter cups. I decided to update that memory in this recipe. I use an almost flourless chocolate cake base instead of pie crust to house the peanut butter filling, then chocolate ganache and candied peanuts push it over the edge. This is a dreamy dessert, and a little goes a long way.

Chocolate Peanut Butter Pie

MAKES · 12 LARGE OR 24 SMALL SQUARES

CHOCOLATE BASE

8 oz [226 g] semisweet or bittersweet chocolate

12 tablespoons [1½ sticks or 170 g] unsalted butter

2 tablespoons Dutch-process cocoa powder

1¼ cups [250 g] granulated sugar

5 large eggs, at room temperature

1 teaspoon pure vanilla extract

¼ teaspoon salt

¼ cup [36 g] all-purpose flour

PEANUT BUTTER FILLING

1½ cups [323 g] creamy peanut butter

4 tablespoons [56 g] unsalted butter, at room temperature

½ cup [60 g] confectioners' sugar

¼ teaspoon salt

1 teaspoon pure vanilla extract

½ teaspoon lemon juice

1¼ cups [300 g] heavy cream

ASSEMBLY

1 recipe Ganache (page 257)

1 cup [140 g] Candied Nuts (page 284), peanut variation

cont'd

34

1) Position an oven rack in the middle of the oven and preheat the oven to 350°F [180°C]. Grease a 9 by 13 in [23 by 33 cm] baking pan and line with a parchment sling. 2) FOR THE CHOCOLATE BASE In a small saucepan over low heat, melt the chocolate and butter, stirring frequently until smooth. Remove from the heat and stir in the cocoa powder. 3) In a large bowl, whisk together the granulated sugar, eggs, vanilla, and salt until smooth. Add the flour and mix again until combined. Add the warm chocolate and whisk until combined. Let the mixture sit for 15 minutes. 4) Pour the batter into the prepared pan and use an offset spatula to smooth the top. Bake until the edges are set and the center jiggles slightly, 15 to 18 minutes. Transfer the pan to a wire rack and let cool completely. 5) FOR THE PEANUT BUTTER FILLING In the bowl of a stand mixer fitted with a paddle, mix together the peanut butter and butter on low speed until smooth and combined, 1 to 2 minutes. Add the confectioners' sugar and salt and

mix again until combined. Add the vanilla and lemon juice and mix again until incorporated. Transfer the mixture to a large bowl and clean out the stand mixer bowl. 6) In the now-clean stand mixer bowl fitted with a whisk, beat the heavy cream on medium speed until soft peaks form, 4 to 5 minutes. Whisk one-third of the whipped cream into the peanut butter mixture to lighten it, then gently fold in the remaining whipped cream. 7) TO ASSEMBLE Dollop the peanut butter mixture over the baked, cooled chocolate base and use an offset spatula to smooth the top, then chill for at least 2 hours and up to 8 hours. Starting in the center of the pie, pour the warm ganache in a steady stream and work your way out to the edge, making sure to completely cover the surface of the pie. Sprinkle the candied peanuts over the top. Transfer the pie to the refrigerator and let chill for 1 hour. 8) Use the parchment sling to gently lift the pie from the pan, cut into squares, and serve. Store in the refrigerator, covered, for up to 2 days.

It's hard to say no to creamy chocolate mousse, especially after a long morning, and Irish cream makes this pretty much irresistible once 3 p.m. hits. If you would prefer to make it without the alcohol, omit the Irish cream from the ganache and use ⅓ cup [80 g] heavy cream instead.

Chocolate Irish Cream Mousse Pie

MAKES · ONE 9 IN
[23 CM] PIE

CRUST

2 cups [200 g] Chocolate Wafer Cookies (page 270) or store-bought (see page 22)

3 tablespoons unsalted butter, melted

IRISH CREAM GANACHE

6 oz [170 g] semisweet or bittersweet chocolate

⅓ cup [80 g] heavy cream

¼ cup [60 g] Irish Cream

CHOCOLATE MOUSSE

2½ cups [600 g] heavy cream

5 large egg yolks, at room temperature

½ cup [100 g] granulated sugar

¼ teaspoon salt

1 teaspoon pure vanilla extract

10 oz [283 g] semisweet or bittersweet chocolate, finely chopped

1 recipe Whipped Cream (page 278) or mascarpone variation (page 279)

35

1) FOR THE CRUST Position an oven rack in the middle of the oven and preheat the oven to 350°F [180°C]. Grease a 9 in [23 cm] springform pan and line with a parchment sling. 2) Place the cookies in the bowl of a food processor and process until broken down into fine crumbs. Transfer the crumbs to a medium bowl and pour the melted butter over the top. Use a spatula to stir together until combined. 3) Press the mixture onto the bottom of the prepared pan and bake for 10 minutes. Let the crust cool completely. 4) FOR THE IRISH CREAM GANACHE Place the chocolate in a small heatproof bowl. In a small saucepan over low heat, heat the heavy cream and Irish cream until simmering and just about to boil. Pour the cream over the chocolate, cover the bowl with plastic wrap, and let sit for 5 minutes.

5) Remove the plastic and whisk until completely smooth. Pour the ganache over the cooled crust and smooth the top with an offset spatula. Transfer the pie to the refrigerator and let the ganache set, about 1 hour. 6) FOR THE CHOCOLATE MOUSSE In a small, heavy saucepan over low heat, heat 1 cup [240 g] of the heavy cream until just hot. 7) In a medium saucepan off the heat, whisk the egg yolks. Whisking constantly, slowly add the granulated sugar to the egg yolks, then the salt, and then slowly pour in the warmed heavy cream. Cook over medium heat, stirring constantly, until the mixture thickens and coats the back of a spoon—this usually happens at 160°F [70°C] (the custard will thicken as it cools). Pour the mixture through a fine-mesh sieve into a large bowl and stir in the vanilla. 8) In a small saucepan over low heat, melt the chocolate, stirring frequently until smooth. Whisk the chocolate into the custard until smooth, then let cool. 9) In the bowl of a stand mixer fitted with a whisk, beat the remaining 1½ cups [360 g] of heavy cream until stiff peaks form. Whisk one-third of the whipped cream into the chocolate custard to lighten it, then gently fold in the remaining whipped cream. 10) Transfer the mousse to the crust over the chilled ganache. Use an offset spatula to spread it in an even layer. Chill the pie for at least 6 hours and up to overnight (I cover the top of the pie with a loose piece of parchment paper. Wrapping it in plastic can make the crust less flaky).

11) When ready to eat, top with the whipped cream and serve. The pie can be stored, covered, in the refrigerator for 24 hours.

Zoë François is known in Minneapolis for a butterscotch pot de crème she created for the restaurant Tilia. In her genius recipe, the butter and brown sugar are cooked together until deep amber and smoking, giving it a unique flavor. I came up with a cheater's method after burning too many batches of sugar; I add a tiny hit of liquid smoke to the pudding instead, and it works like a charm. The liquid smoke can be omitted for classic results, and your pie will be just as delicious.

Smoky Butterscotch Cream Pie

MAKES · ONE 9 IN
[23 CM] PIE

BUTTERSCOTCH FILLING

4 large egg yolks, at room temperature

½ cup [100 g] granulated sugar

½ cup [100 g] brown sugar

1 teaspoon salt

¼ cup [28 g] cornstarch

2 cups [480 g] whole milk

1 cup [240 g] heavy cream

8 tablespoons [1 stick or 113 g] unsalted butter, cut into 1 in [2.5 cm] pieces

1 tablespoon pure vanilla extract

1 tablespoon blackstrap rum or bourbon

A few drops liquid smoke, or more to taste

ASSEMBLY

1 recipe Pat-in-the-Pan Pie Dough (page 262), baked and cooled in a 9 in [23 cm] pie pan

1 recipe Whipped Cream (page 278)

1 cup [140 g] Candied Nuts (page 284), pecan variation, roughly chopped

1) FOR THE BUTTERSCOTCH FILLING In the bowl of a stand mixer fitted with a paddle, beat the egg yolks on low speed. Slowly add the granulated sugar, followed by the brown sugar and salt. Increase the speed to medium and beat until the mixture is thick and pale, about 5 minutes. Scrape down the sides of the bowl and add the cornstarch. Turn the mixer to low speed and mix until combined. 2) In a medium, heavy-bottom saucepan over medium heat, heat the milk and heavy cream until just simmering. Remove from the heat and transfer to a medium liquid measuring cup with a pourable spout. 3) With the mixer running on low speed, very slowly add the hot milk mixture. Mix until completely combined. Return the mixture to the saucepan.

36

4) Cook over low heat, stirring constantly with a wooden spoon, until the mixture becomes thick and begins to boil, 6 to 8 minutes. Switch to a whisk and whisk the mixture until it becomes the consistency of pudding and is glossy, 3 to 4 minutes. Remove the pan from the heat and strain through a fine-mesh sieve into a medium bowl. Stir in the butter, vanilla, rum, and liquid smoke (if using). 5) TO ASSEMBLE Pour the pudding over the cooled crust in the pan and use an offset spatula to smooth the top. Cover with plastic wrap, making sure

the wrap sits directly on top of the pudding (this will help keep it from forming a skin). Chill the pie for at least 6 hours. 6) Top the chilled pie with the whipped cream. Chill the whole pie for at least 1 hour. The pie can be held unsliced in the refrigerator for 8 hours and will keep for up to 2 days, although the crust will not be as crisp as time goes on. Before slicing, top the pie with the candied nuts. The pie is best eaten as soon as possible.

Lemon and white chocolate is a frequent pairing for me—I love the bright, tart flavor of the lemon combined with the extra-sweet chocolate. Here, white chocolate is added to the whipped cream topping, which keeps the flavors slightly more separate and makes for an interesting bite.

Lemon White Chocolate Pie

MAKES • 9 LARGE OR 12 SMALL SQUARES

CRUST

2 cups [200 g] vanilla wafers

5 tablespoons [70 g] unsalted butter, melted

FILLING

4 large egg yolks, at room temperature

½ cup [120 g] lemon juice

2 tablespoons heavy cream

1 tablespoon lemon zest

¼ teaspoon salt

One 14 oz [396 g] can sweetened condensed milk

1 or 2 drops yellow food coloring (optional)

1 recipe Whipped Cream (page 278), white chocolate variation

1 lemon, thinly sliced, for garnishing

1) **FOR THE CRUST** Position an oven rack in the middle of the oven and preheat the oven to 325°F [170°C]. Grease an 8 in [20 cm] square baking pan and line with a parchment sling. 2) In a food processor fitted with a blade, pulse the vanilla wafers until broken down into crumbs. Pour the crumbs into a small bowl, cover with the melted butter, and stir until all the crumbs are coated. Use a measuring cup or the back of a spoon to press the crumbs evenly onto the bottom of the prepared pan. Bake for 10 to 12 minutes, until lightly browned and fragrant. Transfer the pan to a wire rack. 3) **FOR THE FILLING** In a large bowl, whisk together the egg yolks, lemon juice, heavy cream, lemon zest, and salt until combined. Pour in the sweetened condensed milk and whisk again until smooth and fully combined. Add the food coloring (if using) and stir to evenly distribute. Pour the filling over the warm crust. Bake for 14 to 17 minutes, until the center is set but still wiggly when jiggled. 4) Transfer the pie to a wire rack and let cool completely. Place the pan in the refrigerator and chill for at least 4 hours or overnight. Top the chilled pie with the whipped cream and lemon slices, if desired, slice into squares, and serve. The pie can be stored in an airtight container in the refrigerator for 2 days.

37

This pie was inspired by an old-school recipe, Angel Pie, an inside-out version of the classic lemon meringue pie. A meringue shell is used instead of pie crust, and is filled with lemon or lime curd, whipped cream, and/or jam. My version features a poppy seed meringue base cradling lemon curd and a giant pile of whipped cream.

MAKES · 12 LARGE OR
24 SMALL SQUARES

Lemon Meringue Pie

A few drops lemon juice

2 cups [400 g] granulated sugar

1 cup [226 g] egg whites (from 7 or 8 large eggs), at room temperature

¼ teaspoon salt

¼ teaspoon cream of tartar

3 tablespoons poppy seeds

1 tablespoon pure vanilla extract

1 recipe Lemon Curd (page 282)

1 recipe Whipped Cream (page 278)

1) Position an oven rack in the middle of the oven and preheat the oven to 250°F [120°C]. Grease a 9 by 13 in [23 by 33 cm] baking pan and line with a parchment sling. 2) Pour 1 in [2.5 cm] of water into a medium saucepan over medium-high heat and bring to a gentle boil. 3) In the bowl of a stand mixer fitted with a whisk, add the lemon juice and use a paper towel to wipe the juice around the inside of the bowl (this helps remove any trace of grease, which can hinder the whites from whipping properly). Add the sugar, egg whites, salt, and cream of tartar and stir gently with a rubber spatula until completely combined. 4) Place the bowl over the saucepan, being careful not to let the water touch the bottom of the bowl. Stir with the spatula until the sugar is completely dissolved and the mixture registers 160°F [70°C] on an instant-read thermometer, scraping down the sides of the bowl with the spatula (to ensure no sugar crystals are lurking, which can cook the egg whites), 4 to 5 minutes. 5) Place the bowl in the stand mixer and whisk the egg whites on low speed for 1 minute. Slowly increase the speed to medium-high and beat until stiff, glossy peaks form, 8 to 10 minutes. The bowl should feel cool to the touch at this point. Add the poppy seeds and vanilla and mix on low speed until combined.

38

6) Transfer the meringue to the prepared pan, spreading it along the bottom and up the sides of the pan. The sides should be about 1 inch [2.5 cm] higher than the center. Bake the meringue for 2 hours. Turn off the oven and let the meringue sit in the oven for 1 more hour.

7) Transfer the pan to a wire rack to cool completely. Fill the cooled shell with the lemon curd, then top with the whipped cream and use an offset spatula to smooth the top. Chill for 4 hours, then cut into squares and serve. The pie can be stored in an airtight container in the refrigerator for up to 1 day.

I came across "Mock Apple Pie" in a *Saveur* cookbook and took it on as another old-school recipe that I wanted to modernize. The original is said to have been created during the American Civil War, when rations were tight. Crackers were substituted for apples and baked with water, spices, and sugar, for a result that does indeed resemble apple pie filling. In my version, water is replaced with apple cider, I use a dough made with crème fraîche, and I've enriched the filling with more salt, butter, and cinnamon.

Apple Cider Pie

MAKES · 9 LARGE OR
12 SMALL SQUARES

CRUST

All-purpose flour, for dusting

1 recipe Crème Fraîche Dough (page 263)

Egg wash
(see page 16)

Granulated sugar, for sprinkling

FILLING

2 cups [480 g] apple cider

2 cups [400 g] granulated sugar

2 teaspoons cream of tartar

¼ teaspoon salt

2 tablespoons unsalted butter, cut into small pieces

2 tablespoons lemon juice

¾ teaspoon ground cinnamon

2 cups [112 g] crushed saltine crackers (about 36 crackers)

1) **FOR THE CRUST** Grease a 9 in [23 cm] square baking pan and line with a parchment sling. Lightly flour your workspace. Roll one half of the dough into a 9 in [23 cm] square and gently pat it into the bottom of the prepared pan. Roll out the second half of the dough into a 9 in [23 cm] square and place it on a sheet pan lined with parchment paper. Chill both doughs in the refrigerator while making the filling.

2) **FOR THE FILLING** In a large saucepan over medium-high heat, combine the apple cider, granulated sugar, cream of tartar, and salt. Bring the mixture to a boil, then lower the heat to medium-low and let simmer until the mixture starts to thicken and turn syrupy, 13 to 15 minutes. Remove from the heat and stir in the butter, lemon juice, and cinnamon and mix until combined and

the butter has melted. Add the crushed saltines and stir to combine. Let cool for 20 minutes. 3) Fill the prepared shell with the saltine mixture and use an offset spatula to smooth the top. Remove the rolled-out dough from the sheet pan and gently cut a few steam vents in the dough. Place the dough over the top of the filling (no need to press it down to seal the dough). Chill the pan in the refrigerator while the oven preheats. 4) Position an oven rack in the middle of the oven and preheat the oven to 375°F [190°C]. Place a sheet pan on the oven rack (the preheated sheet pan helps crisp the bottom of the pie crust). 5) When ready to bake, brush the top of the pie lightly with the egg wash and sprinkle generously with granulated sugar. Transfer the pie to the preheated sheet pan and bake for 34 to 38 minutes, until the crust is golden brown. Let cool completely before slicing into squares and serving. Apple cider pie is best eaten the same day it is made but can be refrigerated in an airtight container for up to 2 days.

39

40

Each summer, our raspberry bushes are out of control, racing up and down our fence as if they own the place. We adore them, despite their wild tendencies, and I am thankful for the deep pinks and reds peeking out at every turn. Mixed berry pie is always on our list of things to bake, and a little cream cheese tucked into the pie crust helps balance out the tart flavor of the raspberries without having to add piles of extra sugar. I often throw a grated apple in with my pie filling, which adds a little extra pectin as well as sweetness, and using blueberries helps too. Cooking the cornstarch with the strained fruit juices (another trick I learned from Ms. François) helps bind the filling, which makes for a nice, neat slice once cut.

MAKES · 12 LARGE OR
24 SMALL SQUARES

Mixed Berry Cheesecake Slab Pie

CREAM CHEESE FILLING

8 oz [226 g] cream cheese, at room temperature

2 tablespoons granulated sugar

1 tablespoon all-purpose flour

1 large egg, at room temperature

MIXED BERRY FILLING

10 heaping cups [1.3 kg] fresh berries, a mixture of raspberries, blueberries, and/or blackberries (see note, page 122)

1 cup [150 g] peeled and grated Gala apple (about 2 small apples)

¾ cup [150 g] granulated sugar

¼ teaspoon salt

¼ cup [28 g] cornstarch

1 teaspoon lemon juice

2 tablespoons unsalted butter

1 tablespoon raspberry vodka (optional)

1 teaspoon pure vanilla extract

CRUST

All-purpose flour, for dusting

1 recipe Pie Dough (page 261)

Egg wash (see page 16)

Granulated sugar, for sprinkling

cont'd

1) FOR THE CREAM CHEESE FILLING In the bowl of a stand mixer fitted with a paddle, beat the cream cheese on medium speed until smooth and creamy, 2 to 3 minutes. Add the granulated sugar and flour and beat again until smooth. Turn the mixer to low speed, add the egg, and mix until completely combined, stopping to scrape down the sides of the bowl as needed. Refrigerate until ready to use.

2) FOR THE MIXED BERRY FILLING In a large bowl, combine the berries, grated apple, ½ cup [100 g] of the granulated sugar, and salt. Let sit for at least 30 minutes at room temperature. (Letting the fruit sit longer is better, as more juice will be released; 2 hours is a good time frame). 3) Strain the sugary juice from the fruit into a medium saucepan (you should have at least ½ cup [120 g] of juice). Return the fruit to the large bowl and set aside. Add the remaining ¼ cup [50 g] of sugar, the cornstarch, and lemon juice to the juice in the pan and heat over medium heat. Cook until the cornstarch mixture is thick and translucent; the mixture will go from cloudy to shiny and bright. Remove from the heat and whisk in the butter. Stir in the vodka (if using) and vanilla. Set aside to cool slightly. 4) Pour the cornstarch mixture over the berries and stir gently. 5) FOR THE CRUST Lightly flour a large sheet of parchment paper and roll one piece of dough into a 15 by 13 in [41 by 33 cm] rectangle. Repeat with the second piece of dough. Using the parchment paper, transfer one rectangle to a 9 by 13 in [23 by 33 cm] jelly roll pan or quarter sheet pan. Press the dough into the pan and discard the parchment. Pour the berry filling on top of the dough and spread into an even layer. Dollop

the cream cheese filling over the berry filling. Using the parchment paper, place the second rectangle of dough on top of the filling and discard the parchment. Trim the dough overhangs to 1 in [2.5 cm] past the lip of the pan. Pinch the dough together and tuck it under itself. Crimp the edges and cut several X-shaped vents across the top of the dough. Place the pan in the freezer for about 20 minutes while the oven is preheating (you want the crust to be nice and firm before you bake it). 6) Position an oven rack in the lowest position and preheat the oven to 425°F [220°C]. Place a baking sheet large enough to hold the jelly roll pan on the oven rack (the preheated baking sheet helps crisp the bottom of the pie crust and catches any leaks and drips). 7) When ready to bake, brush the top of the slab pie with the egg wash and sprinkle generously with granulated sugar. Place the pie pan on the preheated baking sheet and bake for 25 minutes. Lower the oven temperature to 375°F [190°C] and bake for 35 to 50 minutes more, until the crust is deep golden brown and the juices bubble. Transfer the slab pie in its pan to a wire rack and let cool for at least 4 hours before cutting into portions and serving. The pie is best eaten the same day it is made.

NOTE For a sweeter pie versus a tart pie, use more blueberries than raspberries or blackberries. I usually don't include strawberries in this pie, but if using them, quarter them for best results.

This is my favorite recipe for Key Lime Pie turned on its head—passion fruit replaces the lime, milk chocolate covers the creamy fruit center, and then the whole thing is topped off with toasted meringue. Passion fruit and milk chocolate are a classic combination, but the chocolate ganache can be skipped if you are looking for a straight-up fruit filling.

Passion Fruit S'mores Pie

MAKES · 9 LARGE OR 12 SMALL BARS

CRUST

1½ cups [150 g] graham cracker crumbs

1 tablespoon granulated sugar

5 tablespoons [70 g] unsalted butter, melted and cooled

8 oz [226 g] milk chocolate, chopped

FILLING

4 large egg yolks

¾ cup [180 g] passion fruit concentrate

½ teaspoon pure vanilla extract

¼ teaspoon salt

One 14 oz [396 g] can sweetened condensed milk

1 recipe Meringue (page 258)

1) FOR THE CRUST Position an oven rack in the middle of the oven and preheat the oven to 325°F [170°C]. Grease an 8 in [20 cm] square baking pan and line with a parchment sling. **2)** Place the graham cracker crumbs in a medium bowl and whisk in the granulated sugar. Pour the melted butter over the top, then use a spatula to stir together until combined. **3)** Transfer to the prepared pan and use a measuring cup or spoon to press the crumbs evenly onto the bottom of the pan. Bake for 12 to 15 minutes, until brown and fragrant. Remove the pan from the oven, scatter the milk chocolate evenly over the crust, and bake for 2 minutes. Use the back of a spoon to spread the chocolate smoothly over the crust. Transfer the pan to a wire rack and let cool slightly.

cont'd

4) FOR THE FILLING In a large bowl, whisk together the egg yolks, passion fruit concentrate, vanilla, and salt until combined. Pour in the sweetened condensed milk and whisk again until smooth and fully combined. Pour the filling over the warm crust. 5) Bake for 14 to 17 minutes, until the center is set when jiggled. Transfer the pan to a wire rack and let cool to room temperature. Chill the bars for 4 hours or overnight. 6) TO ASSEMBLE Make the meringue as directed. Working quickly, pile the meringue on top of the chilled filling. Use an offset spatula to spread the meringue evenly over the top. Use a kitchen torch to carefully brown the meringue. Slice the pie into squares and serve. Store covered, in the refrigerator for up to 2 days.

I wanted a summer pie that highlighted strawberries but didn't require a labor-intensive pie crust or gelatin. Graham cracker crumbs and whipped cream were the obvious choices, but roasted strawberries were the key. The intense flavor and juices from the berries made this pie special, and swirling some of the mashed, roasted berries into the whipped cream helped this pie scream of strawberries. A perfect dessert for long summer afternoons.

Roasted Strawberry Cream Pie

MAKES · ONE 9 IN [23 CM] PIE

42

CRUST

2 cups [200 g] graham cracker crumbs

1 tablespoon granulated sugar

4 tablespoons [56 g] unsalted butter, melted

STRAWBERRIES

2 lb [900 g] strawberries, hulled

2 tablespoons granulated sugar

Pinch of salt

1 vanilla bean, split (optional)

1 tablespoon strawberry schnapps

1 recipe Whipped Cream (page 278), mascarpone variation

1) Position an oven rack in the middle of the oven and preheat the oven to 325°F [170°C]. 2) FOR THE CRUST In a medium bowl, mix together the graham cracker crumbs and granulated sugar. Add the melted butter and stir until all the crumbs are coated. Use a measuring cup or spoon to press the crumbs evenly into the bottom and up the sides of a 9 in [23 cm] pie pan. 3) Bake for 12 to 15 minutes, until lightly browned and fragrant. Transfer the pan to a wire rack and let cool. 4) FOR THE ROASTED STRAW-BERRIES Increase the oven temperature to 400°F [200°C]. 5) In a large baking dish, combine the strawberries, granulated sugar, and salt and toss to combine. Nestle the vanilla bean (if using) into the strawberries.

cont'd

6) Bake, uncovered, until the strawberries are tender and are leaking juices, 20 to 25 minutes. Transfer the pan to a wire rack and let the berries cool to room temperature. Remove the vanilla bean and save for another application or discard. 7) TO ASSEMBLE In a small bowl, mash 1 cup of the roasted berries with a fork. Stir the mashed berries and strawberry schnapps into the mascarpone whipped cream.

8) Scatter 1 cup of the roasted berries on the bottom of the cooled pie shell. Pour the mascarpone whipped cream over the berries, then top with the remaining roasted berries. This pie is best served immediately, but can be stored in the refrigerator, covered, for up to 1 day.

I make these streusel bars every holiday season; the brown-buttered crumbly streusel pairs seamlessly with the creamy pumpkin filling, and the cinnamon, ginger, and cloves give off late November vibes. Regardless, my kids often beg for them in the middle of July, and if I find you baking them in the summer months too, I will absolutely understand.

MAKES · 12 LARGE OR 24 SMALL BARS

Pumpkin Streusel Pie

PUMPKIN FILLING

One 15 oz [425 g] can unsweetened pumpkin purée

One 14 oz [396 g] can sweetened condensed milk

2 large eggs, at room temperature

2 tablespoons brown sugar

1 teaspoon pure vanilla extract

1 teaspoon ground cinnamon

¾ teaspoon ground ginger

¾ teaspoon salt

¼ teaspoon ground nutmeg

Pinch of cloves

CRUST

1 cup [2 sticks or 227 g] unsalted butter, at room temperature, cut into ½ in [13 mm] slices

2¾ cups [391 g] all-purpose flour

1 cup [200 g] granulated sugar

¼ cup [25 g] almond flour or quick oats

½ teaspoon baking powder

½ teaspoon salt

1 large egg, at room temperature

43

1) Position an oven rack in the middle of the oven and preheat the oven to 350°F [180°C]. Grease a 9 by 13 in [23 by 33 cm] baking pan and line with a parchment sling. 2) FOR THE PUMPKIN FILLING In a large bowl, whisk together the pumpkin purée, sweetened condensed milk, eggs, brown sugar, vanilla, cinnamon, ginger, salt, nutmeg, and cloves until smooth. Set aside. 3) FOR THE CRUST Melt 8 tablespoons [113 g] of the butter in a medium skillet over medium-high heat. Brown the butter until it is dark golden brown and is giving off a nutty aroma, 2 to 3 minutes (for tips on browning butter, see page 276). Pour the browned butter (and any bits of browned butter stuck to the bottom of the skillet) into a medium bowl and let cool for 10 minutes.

cont'd

4) In the bowl of a stand mixer fitted with a paddle, combine the all-purpose flour, granulated sugar, almond flour, baking powder, and salt. Add the browned butter and mix on low speed until the butter is combined into the flour mixture. Add the egg and mix again until the egg is worked into the flour. Add the remaining 8 tablespoons [113 g] butter to the flour and mix until the butter is combined and the mixture is crumbly. 5) Press half of the crust mixture into the bottom of the prepared pan. 6) Bake for 10 minutes. Spread the pumpkin mixture over the crust, sprinkle the remaining crust mixture evenly over the top, and bake for 18 to 25 more minutes, until the pumpkin has puffed up a bit and does not jiggle, and the crumbly top is light golden brown. 7) Transfer the pan to a wire rack and let cool. Place the pan in the refrigerator and chill for 4 to 6 hours. Slice into bars and serve. The bars can be served cold or at room temperature but keep best in an airtight container in the refrigerator for about 3 days.

In Minnesota, rhubarb's ruby red appearance is the whisper that spring has finally arrived, and what I like to think Emily Dickinson is referencing: "A Light exists in spring... a color stands abroad / on solitary hills / That science cannot overtake, / But human nature feels." With such a dramatic entrance, it's important for every Northern baker to have good rhubarb recipes in her baking tool belt. I like to balance the very tart rhubarb with sugar and cream, and in these hand pies I make a rhubarb jam that pairs beautifully with creamy mascarpone, which I wrap up in flaky, buttery puff pastry.

Rhubarb and Cream Hand Pies

MAKES · 8 HAND PIES

RHUBARB JAM

2 cups [250 g] chopped rhubarb, fresh or frozen, cut into 1 in [2.5 cm] pieces

½ cup [100 g] granulated sugar

1 teaspoon lemon juice

¼ teaspoon salt

1 teaspoon pure vanilla extract

MASCARPONE FILLING

2 oz [57 g] cream cheese, at room temperature

2 oz [57 g] mascarpone cheese, at room temperature

¼ cup [50 g] granulated sugar

ASSEMBLY

All-purpose flour, for dusting

1 recipe Rough Puff Pastry (page 268), cut into 2 pieces

Water, for brushing

Egg wash (see page 16)

Granulated sugar, for sprinkling

1) **FOR THE RHUBARB JAM** In a medium saucepan over medium heat, combine the rhubarb, granulated sugar, lemon juice, and salt and simmer, stirring often, for 20 to 30 minutes, until the rhubarb has broken down and the jam is thick enough to coat a wooden spoon.

cont'd

44

2) Remove the pan from the heat, stir in the vanilla, and let cool to room temperature.
3) FOR THE MASCARPONE FILLING In the bowl of a stand mixer fitted with a paddle, beat the cream cheese and mascarpone cheese on medium speed until smooth. Scrape down the sides of the bowl and add the granulated sugar, mixing on low speed until completely combined. Transfer to a small bowl and refrigerate until ready to use. 4) TO ASSEMBLE Line a sheet pan with parchment paper. 5) Generously flour your work surface. Roll one piece of the pastry dough into a 10 in [25 cm] square. Cut into four 5 in [12 cm] squares. Repeat with the second piece of dough, for a total of eight squares. Place a dollop of jam and a dollop of mascarpone filling on each square, about 1 tablespoon of each. Brush the edges of each square lightly with water, fold the dough to make a triangle, and crimp the edges with a fork to seal.

6) Transfer the triangles to the prepared sheet pan and place in the freezer while the oven preheats. 7) Position an oven rack in the middle of the oven and preheat the oven to 400°F [200°C]. 8) Brush the tops of the hand pies lightly with egg wash and generously sprinkle with granulated sugar. Slide another sheet pan underneath so the pans are double stacked (this helps keep the bottoms from overbrowning). Bake the pies until golden brown, rotating the pan halfway through baking, 20 to 25 minutes. Remove from the oven and use a spatula to transfer the pies to a wire rack to cool slightly. Serve warm. Hand pies are best eaten the same day they are made.

NOTE You will have some rhubarb jam leftover; this tastes delicious on toast.

I make this version of banana cream pie in small containers for several reasons: It is easy to serve them packaged this way, I don't have to mess with gelatin in my filling to set the banana pastry cream, and these elevated pudding cups are the best way to spend an afternoon. If you can splurge on a vanilla bean to use in the pastry cream, you won't regret it.

Banana Cream Pie

MAKES · 6 SERVINGS

CRUST

2 cups [200 g] graham cracker crumbs or Nilla Wafer crumbs

1 tablespoon granulated sugar

4 tablespoons [56 g] unsalted butter, melted

ASSEMBLY

1 recipe Pastry Cream (page 279)

2½ cups [400 g] bananas, sliced into ¼ in [6 mm] circles (about 4 bananas)

1 recipe Whipped Cream (page 278), mascarpone variation

Candied Nuts (page 284), Candied Cacao Nibs (page 288), or chocolate curls (optional)

45

1) Position an oven rack in the middle of the oven and preheat the oven to 325°F [170°C]. Line a sheet pan with parchment paper. 2) In a medium bowl, mix together the graham cracker crumbs and granulated sugar. Pour the melted butter over the top and stir until all the crumbs are coated. Pour the crumbs onto the prepared sheet pan and spread into an even layer. 3) Bake the crumbs until golden and fragrant, 12 to 15 minutes. Transfer the pan to a wire rack and let cool to room temperature. 4) TO ASSEMBLE In a large bowl, stir together the pastry cream and the bananas until combined.

5) Divide the cooled graham cracker crumbs between six 3 by 2 in [7.5 by 5 cm] ramekins or other similar-size vessels, pressing them down on the bottom to form an even layer. Divide the pastry cream among the ramekins, then top each one with the mascarpone whipped cream. Chill the pies for 1 hour and up to 8 hours before serving. Top with candied nuts, candied cacao nibs, or chocolate curls (if using).

NOTE Bananas can turn brown in the pastry cream if sitting for more than a few hours. Some bakers brush their banana slices with lemon juice to help slow the browning process, but this can change the flavor of the pie and it's not ideal. You can also wait until just before serving to mix the bananas into the pastry cream. I think the flavor is best when the bananas sit in the cream for a few hours, and just serve as is.

CHAPTER 4

No Bakes

"They might not
need me—
yet they might—

I'll let my Heart
be just in sight."

—Emily Dickinson

Chocolate and mint is a special flavor combination for me, not only because I think it is delicious (which it is) but because it was my ice cream of choice growing up. Once a month when my sister and I were still in the single digits, my grandma would pick us up on a Friday afternoon and take us to her house for a sleepover. She would always stop at the grocery store and let us pick out dinner and treats: Salisbury steak TV dinners and cheese and crackers for me (my sister always chose cottage cheese, buttermilk, and black olives for her snacks, and I refused to sit by her while she ate them). We also got to pick out a small pint of ice cream, and peppermint bonbon was what I reached for. These mint and chocolate bars aren't quite the same as that little pint, but they never fail to remind me of those Friday nights.

Mint Chocolate Ice Cream Bars

MAKES · 9 LARGE OR 12 SMALL BARS

One 14 oz [396 g] can sweetened condensed milk

1 tablespoon crème de menthe (optional)

1 to 2 teaspoons mint extract, or to taste

1 teaspoon pure vanilla extract

¼ teaspoon salt

2 oz [57 g] cream cheese, at room temperature

2½ cups [600 g] heavy cream

48 chocolate sandwich cookies, such as Oreos or Oreo Thins (see note, page 139)

1) In a large bowl, whisk together the sweetened condensed milk, crème de menthe (if using), mint extract, vanilla, and salt until completely combined. 2) In the bowl of a stand mixer fitted with a whisk, beat the cream cheese on medium speed until smooth, 5 to 6 minutes. Turn the mixer to low speed and add the heavy cream in a slow, steady stream, mixing until combined. Increase the speed to medium and whisk until stiff peaks form, 3 to 4 minutes.

3) Add half of the whipped cream mixture to the sweetened condensed milk mixture and whisk until completely combined. Using a rubber spatula, gently fold in the remaining whipped cream mixture until no streaks remain.

4) Grease an 8 in [20 cm] square baking pan or 9 in [23 cm] square baking pan and line with a parchment sling. Pour two-thirds of the cream mixture into the prepared pan. Gently press the chocolate cookies vertically into the ice cream, about 1 in [2.5 cm] apart, lining them up in rows; you will get about 4 rows of 13 cookies. Pour the remaining cream mixture over the top and use an offset spatula to smooth the top. Freeze until firm, 8 hours or overnight. When ready to serve, remove the ice cream with the parchment sling and cut into squares. Eat immediately. The bars can be stored in the freezer, covered, for up to 1 week.

NOTE You may be able to squeeze more or fewer cookies into the rows in the ice cream depending on your pan size and how close together you want them. You can also use the Chocolate Wafer Cookies, page 270, instead of the Oreos if desired.

Red velvet is more red food coloring than chocolate, and while on paper that may not seem appealing, there is something enticing about the ruby hue against bright-white cream cheese buttercream that has made it a classic. Here's my ice cream version, complete with cream cheese swirls and cookie crunch.

MAKES · ONE 9 IN [23 CM] CAKE

Red Velvet Ice Cream Cake

CREAM CHEESE SWIRL

7 oz [198 g] cream cheese, at room temperature

½ cup [100 g] granulated sugar

2 tablespoons heavy cream

Pinch of salt

CRUST

20 chocolate sandwich cookies [238 g], such as Oreos

4 tablespoons [56 g] unsalted butter, melted

COOKIE CRUMBLE

12 chocolate sandwich cookies [137 g], such as Oreos

¼ cup [70 g] Chocolate Magic Shell (page 288), warm

ICE CREAM

One 14 oz [396 g] can sweetened condensed milk

2 tablespoons Dutch-process cocoa powder

1 tablespoon red food coloring

1 teaspoon pure vanilla extract

¼ teaspoon salt

2½ cups [600 g] heavy cream

1) FOR THE CREAM CHEESE SWIRL In a medium bowl, mix together the cream cheese, granulated sugar, heavy cream, and salt until combined, then whisk until smooth and creamy. Refrigerate until ready to use. 2) FOR THE CRUST Grease a 9 in [23 cm] springform pan and line with a parchment sling. 3) In the bowl of a food processor fitted with a blade, pulse the chocolate cookies until broken down into crumbs. Pour the cookie crumbs into a medium bowl, then add the melted butter and stir until all the crumbs are coated. Pour into a large skillet and heat over medium heat, stirring frequently, until the crumbs are lightly toasted and fragrant (see note, page 144). 4) Pour the crumbs into the prepared pan. Use a measuring cup or spoon to press the crumbs evenly into the bottom of the pan.

5) FOR THE COOKIE CRUMBLE In the bowl of a food processor fitted with a blade, pulse the chocolate cookies until broken down into crumbs. Pour the cookie crumbs into a medium bowl and coat with the warm magic shell, tossing with a spatula until the cookies are all covered. **6) FOR THE ICE CREAM** In a large bowl, whisk together the sweetened condensed milk, cocoa powder, food coloring, vanilla, and salt until completely combined. **7)** In the bowl of a stand mixer fitted with a whisk, whisk the heavy cream on medium speed until stiff peaks form, 5 to 6 minutes. **8)** Add half of the whipped cream mixture to the sweet-ened condensed milk mixture and whisk until completely combined. Using a rubber spatula, gently fold in the remaining whipped cream mixture until no streaks remain. **9)** Top the crumbs in the pan with half of the red velvet ice

47

cream. Dollop half of the cream cheese mixture over the top and use a butter knife to swirl the cream cheese into the ice cream. Sprinkle the cookie crumble evenly over the top. Cover with the remaining ice cream and repeat swirling with the remaining cream cheese mixture. Place the ice cream cake in the freezer and freeze for at least 8 hours or overnight. **10)** Remove the cake from the pan with the parchment sling and set the cake on a serving platter. Slice and serve immediately. The cake can be stored in the freezer, covered, for up to 1 week.

This cake is a showstopper, and a perfect ice cream treat to serve around the holidays. There is much room for interpretation, however, and any of the No-Churn Ice Cream flavors (page 283) can be swapped in for everyday afternoon ice cream cake snacking. (I particularly like replacing the pumpkin with the coffee-flavored ice cream.)

MAKES · ONE 9 IN [23 CM] LOAF CAKE

Pumpkin Caramel Ice Cream Cake

48

CRUST

1½ cups [150 g] store-bought cinnamon graham cracker crumbs

4 tablespoons [56 g] unsalted butter, melted

ICE CREAM CAKE

1 recipe No-Churn Ice Cream (page 283), salted caramel variation

1 recipe No-Churn Ice Cream (page 283), pumpkin variation

ASSEMBLY

1 recipe Meringue (page 258)

1) Grease a 9 by 4 in [23 by 10 cm] Pullman pan and line with a parchment sling. **2)** FOR THE CRUST In the bowl of a food processor fitted with a blade, pulse the graham crackers until broken down into crumbs. Pour into a medium bowl, then add the melted butter and stir until all the crumbs are coated. Pour into a large skillet and heat over medium heat, stirring frequently, until the crumbs are lightly toasted and fragrant (see note, page 144). **3)** Pour half of the crumbs into the prepared pan. Use a measuring cup or spoon to press the crumbs evenly into the bottom of the pan. Let cool to room temperature.

cont'd

4) FOR THE ICE CREAM CAKE Make the salted caramel ice cream as directed on page 284, and pour a little over half of it into the pan; you want the ice cream to come halfway up the pan. Sprinkle the top with the remaining crumbs, then freeze until firm, about 2 hours. Make the pumpkin ice cream as directed on page 284, and pour enough into the pan until it is almost to the top. Place the ice cream cake in the freezer and freeze for at least 8 hours or overnight. The remaining ice cream can be poured into separate containers and frozen.

5) TO ASSEMBLE Use the parchment sling to gently remove the cake from the loaf pan. Working quickly, remove the parchment paper and set the cake on a serving platter. Use a spatula to spread the meringue evenly over the top of the ice cream cake and, if desired, use a spoon to create swirls. Hold a kitchen torch 1 to 2 in [2.5 to 5 cm] away from the cake and touch the flame down in between the swirls; they will toast and brown (if the swirls catch on fire, blow them out). Slice and serve immediately. The cake can be stored in the freezer, covered, for up to 3 days.

NOTE In order to keep these recipes no-bake, I use the stovetop to toast the cookie-crumb crust in several recipes. If you would prefer to use the oven for this step, you can! Press the cookie crust into the prepared pan and bake at 325°F [170°C] until golden and fragrant.

A twist on the classic strawberry shortcake: frozen shortcake with balsamic vinegar. The vinegar adds flavor and balances the sweetness, while the sandwich cookies stand in for the cake base.

Strawberry Balsamic Shortcake Ice Cream Bars

MAKES · 9 LARGE
OR 12 SMALL BARS

1 lb [455 g] fresh strawberries, hulled and sliced, plus more for decorating

¼ cup [16 g] freeze-dried strawberry powder (see page 16)

1 tablespoon granulated sugar

1 tablespoon balsamic vinegar, plus more to taste

2 tablespoons strawberry vodka (optional)

1 tablespoon pure vanilla extract

One 14 oz [396 g] can sweetened condensed milk

¼ teaspoon salt

2 oz [57 g] cream cheese, at room temperature

2½ cups [600 g] heavy cream

1 or 2 drops pink food coloring (optional)

48 vanilla sandwich cookies, such as Golden Oreos or Golden Oreo Thins (see note, page 147)

1 recipe Whipped Cream (page 278)

1) In a medium saucepan over medium heat, bring the strawberries, freeze-dried strawberry powder, granulated sugar, and balsamic vinegar to a simmer. Cook for about 5 minutes, stirring frequently and mashing the berries slightly, until they have released their juices. Remove from the heat and stir in the vodka (if using) and vanilla. Let cool to room temperature. 2) In a large bowl, whisk together the sweetened condensed milk and salt until completely combined. Stir in the cooled strawberry mixture.

cont'd

49

3) In the bowl of a stand mixer fitted with a whisk, beat the cream cheese on medium speed until smooth. Turn the mixer to low speed and add the heavy cream in a slow, steady stream, mixing until combined. Increase the speed to medium and whisk until stiff peaks form, 3 to 4 minutes. 4) Add half of the cream mixture to the sweetened condensed milk mixture and whisk until completely combined. Using a rubber spatula, gently fold in the remaining cream mixture until no streaks remain. Stir in the food coloring (if using). 5) Line an 8 in [20 cm] square baking pan or 9 in [23 cm] square baking pan with a parchment sling. Pour two-thirds of the ice cream into the prepared pan. Gently press the cookies vertically into the ice cream, about 1 in [2.5 cm] apart, lining them up in rows. You will get about 4 rows of 13 cookies. Pour the remaining ice cream over the top and use an offset spatula to smooth the top. Freeze until firm, 8 hours or overnight. 6) When ready to serve, remove the bars with the parchment sling and cut into squares. Top each piece with some of the whipped cream and fresh strawberries. Eat immediately. The bars can be stored in the freezer, covered, for up to 3 days.

NOTE You may be able to squeeze more or fewer cookies into the ice cream depending on your pan size and how close together you want them.

Elementary school was the first time I ever tried Neapolitan ice cream. My sister and I were upstairs at my grandma's house, trying to ignore both the football game blasting from her TV and the cries of my three-month-old brother, who was exhausted after the long drive. My grandma had just yelled at us for the fourth time for being too loud, and we were horribly offended, as we couldn't possibly be louder than the noise coming from the living room (the jury is still out on this). My dad passed us ice cream bars with a wink of solidarity, and I had never seen anything so beautiful: vanilla, strawberry, and chocolate, all in one rectangle. I quickly forgave my family with each bite, and my sister and I agreed that this was the best ice cream we had ever had.

MAKES · 12 LARGE OR
16 SMALL BARS

Neapolitan Ice Cream Bars

CRUST

2 cups [200 g] Chocolate Wafer Cookies (page 270) or store-bought (see page 22)

5 tablespoons [70 g] unsalted butter, melted

ICE CREAM

One 14 oz [396 g] can sweetened condensed milk

1 tablespoon pure vanilla extract

¼ teaspoon salt

¼ cup [16 g] freeze-dried strawberry powder (see page 16)

2 oz [57 g] cream cheese, at room temperature

2½ cups [600 g] heavy cream

1 recipe Chocolate Magic Shell (page 288), warm

1) FOR THE CRUST Grease an 8 in [20 cm] square baking pan or 9 in [23 cm] square baking pan and line with a parchment sling. 2) In the bowl of a food processor fitted with a blade, pulse the chocolate cookies until broken down into crumbs. Pour into a medium bowl, then add the melted butter and stir until all the crumbs are coated. Pour into a large skillet and heat over medium heat, stirring frequently, until the crumbs are lightly toasted and fragrant (see note, page 144). 3) Pour the crumbs into the prepared pan. Use a measuring cup or spoon to press the crumbs evenly

50

into the bottom of the pan. Let cool to room temperature. 4) FOR THE ICE CREAM In a large bowl, whisk together the sweetened condensed milk, vanilla, and salt until completely combined. Pour half of the mixture into another large bowl. Add the freeze-dried strawberry powder to the second bowl and whisk to combine. 5) In the bowl of a stand mixer fitted with a whisk, beat the cream cheese on medium speed until smooth. Turn the mixer to low speed and add the heavy cream in a slow, steady stream, mixing until combined. Increase the speed to medium and whisk until stiff peaks form, 3 to 4 minutes. Divide the whipped cream between the two bowls and use a rubber spatula to gently fold it into each mixture until no streaks remain. 6) Pour the vanilla ice cream mixture over the prepared crust and smooth the top with the back of a spoon or an offset spatula. Pour the strawberry mixture over the top of the vanilla and use a butter knife to swirl a figure-eight motion, if desired (this step can be omitted for more distinct layers). Freeze the bars until firm, 6 hours or overnight. 7) When ready to serve, remove the bars with the parchment sling and cut into squares. Top each piece with some of the warm magic shell and serve immediately. The bars can be stored in the freezer, covered, for up to 1 week.

51

I love passion fruit and wanted to come up with a dessert that highlighted its bold, refreshing flavor while also taming some of its acidity. The sugar and heavy cream help balance out some bitter notes in the passion fruit while also bringing forward its unique sweet-and-sour flavor. This slice is perfect for hot summer afternoons.

Passion Fruit Slice

MAKES · 12 LARGE OR
16 SMALL SLICES

¾ cup [150 g] granulated sugar

¼ teaspoon salt

½ cup [120 g] passion fruit purée

2½ cups [600 g] heavy whipping cream

Passion fruit pulp from 2 passion fruits (optional)

1) Line a 9 by 4 in [23 by 10 cm] Pullman pan with a parchment sling. 2) In the bowl of a food processor fitted with a blade, pulse the granulated sugar and salt until the sugar is broken down into fine crystals, about 1 minute. Add the passion fruit purée and pulse again until combined, 20 seconds. 3) With the motor running, pour the heavy cream through the feed tube. Process just until the cream thickens into whipped cream. Use a spatula to stir in the passion fruit pulp (if using), then pour the mixture into the prepared pan, using an offset spatula or the back of a spoon to smooth the top. Freeze for at least 8 hours or overnight. 4) When ready to serve, use the parchment sling to remove the fruit slice from the pan, then slice and serve immediately. The slices can be stored in the freezer, covered, for up to 1 week.

Rice Krispies bars are my kryptonite. Something about all their components combined—soft but crunchy, sweet but salty—make them irresistible to me. I take them one step further here with this kitchen sink version, adding even more to these crispy and salty indulgences.

Kitchen Sink Crispy Treats

MAKES · 9 LARGE OR 12 SMALL BARS

8 tablespoons [1 stick or 113 g] unsalted butter

1 cup [215 g] creamy peanut butter

½ teaspoon salt

One 10 oz [283 g] bag plus 2 cups [100 g] mini marshmallows

⅓ cup [57 g] butterscotch chips

1 tablespoon pure vanilla extract

1 tablespoon bourbon (optional)

6 cups [180 g] Rice Krispies cereal

1 cup [35 g] kettle-cooked potato chips, lightly crushed

⅓ cup [57 g] semisweet chocolate chips

2 tablespoons cacao nibs

1) Grease an 8 in [20 cm] square baking pan and line with parchment. 2) In a large, heavy-bottom saucepan, brown the butter (for tips on browning butter, see page 276). Over low heat, add the peanut butter and salt and stir until smooth. Add the marshmallows and heat over medium heat until all the marshmallows are melted. Add the butterscotch chips and stir until smooth. 3) Remove the pan from the heat and stir in the vanilla and bourbon (if using). Add the cereal and potato chips and stir until combined, then add the chocolate chips and cacao nibs, stirring to combine.

4) Transfer the mixture to the prepared pan and flatten the mixture with your (greased) hands or the back of a measuring cup. 5) Let the bars set at room temperature, about 1 hour, and then use the parchment sling to lift them out of the pan. Slice into squares and serve. The bars can be stored in an airtight container at room temperature for up to 2 days.

I love making cheesecake, and this no-bake version makes the task almost easy, along with no risk of the cake cracking or not setting. This chocolate version is rich and creamy, and can be passed off as both a celebration cake or the ultimate afternoon indulgence.

Chocolate Cheesecake

MAKES · ONE 9 IN
[23 CM] CAKE

CRUST

2 cups [200 g] Chocolate Wafer Cookies (page 270) or store-bought (see page 22)

2 tablespoons cacao nibs

5 tablespoons [70 g] unsalted butter, melted

CHEESECAKE FILLING

2 lb [900 g] cream cheese, at room temperature

1 cup [200 g] granulated sugar

¼ teaspoon salt

2 teaspoons pure vanilla extract

8 oz [226 g] semisweet chocolate, melted and cooled

¾ cup [180 g] heavy cream

GLAZE

6 oz [170 g] semisweet or bittersweet chocolate, finely chopped

¾ cup [180 g] heavy cream

1) FOR THE CRUST Grease a 9 in [23 cm] baking pan and line with a parchment sling. **2)** In the bowl of a food processor fitted with a blade, pulse the chocolate cookies and cacao nibs until broken down into crumbs. Pour into a medium bowl, then add the melted butter and stir until all the crumbs are coated. Pour into a large skillet and heat over medium heat, stirring frequently, until the crumbs are lightly toasted and fragrant (see note, page 144). Pour the crumbs into the prepared pan. Use a measuring cup or spoon to press the crumbs evenly into the bottom of the pan. **3) FOR THE CHEESECAKE FILLING** In the bowl of a stand mixer fitted with a paddle, beat the cream cheese on high speed until smooth and creamy, about 3 minutes. Add the granulated sugar and salt and

53

beat again on medium speed until light and smooth, 3 to 4 minutes. Scrape down the sides of the bowl, add the vanilla, and mix again until combined. Add the chocolate and mix again until completely combined and smooth. Transfer the cream cheese mixture to a large bowl and set aside. 4) In the bowl of a stand mixer fitted with a whisk (it's okay to use the same bowl), beat the heavy cream on low speed for 30 to 45 seconds. Increase the speed to medium and continue beating until soft peaks form, 3 to 5 minutes. 5) With a rubber spatula, stir half of the whipped cream mixture into the cream cheese mixture and fold until combined. Add the remaining whipped cream and gently fold again until combined and no streaks remain. 6) Pour the filling over the cookie crust in the pan and use an offset spatula to smooth the top. Refrigerate the cheesecake until firm, at

least 8 hours or overnight. 7) FOR THE GLAZE Place the chocolate in a small heatproof bowl. In a small saucepan over low heat, heat the heavy cream until it is simmering and just about to boil. Pour the cream over the chocolate, cover the bowl with plastic wrap, and let sit for 5 minutes. 8) Remove the plastic wrap and stir the chocolate into the cream until completely smooth. 9) Pour the chocolate glaze over the top of the chilled cheesecake, right in the center. Using an offset spatula, cover the whole top with the glaze, carefully smoothing it out as you move it to the edges. Refrigerate the cheesecake for 1 hour. When ready to serve, cut into squares. The cake can be stored in the refrigerator, covered, for up to 2 days.

This recipe has been around forever with a million different spins on it. Nevertheless, here is my take, because I love these peanut butter and chocolate squares. I use both graham cracker crumbs and corn flakes in the filling, for extra crunch and a salty balance to the confectioners' sugar. These are dangerous—but delicious.

Peanut Butter Chocolate Bars

MAKES · 9 LARGE OR 12 SMALL BARS

BARS

6 tablespoons [84 g] unsalted butter, at room temperature

⅓ cup [65 g] brown sugar

½ teaspoon salt

1⅓ cups [285 g] creamy peanut butter

1 teaspoon pure vanilla extract

1 cup [30 g] corn flakes

½ cup [50 g] graham cracker crumbs

1¼ cups [150 g] confectioners' sugar

GLAZE

8 oz [226 g] semisweet or bittersweet chocolate

⅓ cup [80 g] heavy cream

2 tablespoons corn syrup

1) FOR THE BARS Grease an 8 in [20 cm] square baking pan and line with a parchment sling. 2) In the bowl of a stand mixer fitted with a paddle, beat the butter until creamy, about 1 minute. Add the brown sugar and salt and beat to combine, then add the peanut butter and vanilla and beat until combined and creamy, 2 to 3 minutes. Add the corn flakes and graham cracker crumbs and mix again until combined. Add the confectioner's sugar and mix until completely combined. 3) Transfer the peanut butter mixture to the prepared pan and gently press it into the pan, covering the whole surface. Use your hands or the bottom of a measuring cup to even out the top. Chill the bars for 1 hour.

4) FOR THE GLAZE Place the chocolate in a small heatproof bowl. In a small saucepan over medium heat, heat the heavy cream until it is simmering and just about to boil. Pour the cream over the chocolate, cover the bowl with plastic wrap, and let sit for 5 minutes.

5) Remove the plastic wrap, add the corn syrup, and stir the chocolate into the cream until completely smooth.

6) Pour the glaze over the chilled peanut butter bars and use an offset spatula to smooth the glaze evenly. Chill the bars again for 1 hour. Slice the bars into squares and serve. The bars can be stored in an airtight container in the refrigerator for up to 3 days.

54

Ever since my youth, s'mores have been a disaster for me: overly burnt marshmallows, un-melted chocolate, and graham cracker pieces flying everywhere that first bite. I wanted to give you a s'mores bar that had a soft, toasty marshmallow filling, a rich, creamy chocolate top, and a manageable crunch. Here cream and marshmallows cook down and chill into a squidgy center for a nostalgic, but less messy, bite.

S'mores Bars

MAKES · 9 LARGE
OR 12 SMALL BARS

CRUST

1½ cups [150 g] graham cracker crumbs

1 tablespoon granulated sugar

4 tablespoons [56 g] unsalted butter, melted

FILLING

4 oz [113 g] cream cheese, at room temperature

¼ cup [50 g] granulated sugar

1½ cups [360 g] heavy cream

One 10 oz [283 g] bag mini marshmallows, plus 1 cup [50 g] mini marshmallows

¼ teaspoon salt

1 tablespoon pure vanilla extract

CHOCOLATE GLAZE

6 oz [170 g] semisweet or bittersweet chocolate

⅓ cup [80 g] heavy cream

2 tablespoons corn syrup

1) **FOR THE CRUST** Grease a 9 in [23 cm] square baking pan and line with a parchment sling. 2) In a medium bowl, mix together the graham cracker crumbs and granulated sugar. Add the melted butter and stir until all the crumbs are coated. Pour into a large skillet and heat over medium heat, stirring frequently, until the crumbs are lightly toasted and fragrant (see note, page 144). 3) Pour the crumbs into the prepared pan. Use a measuring cup or spoon to press the crumbs evenly onto the bottom of the pan.

cont'd

4) FOR THE FILLING In the bowl of a stand mixer fitted with a paddle, beat the cream cheese on medium speed until smooth. Add the granulated sugar and beat on low speed until combined, then increase the speed to medium and beat until smooth, 3 or 4 minutes. Scrape down the sides of the bowl and switch to the whisk. With the mixer running on low speed, slowly add 1 cup [240 g] of the heavy cream and whisk until fully combined. Increase the speed to medium and beat for 2 to 3 minutes, until stiff peaks form, stopping to scrape down the sides of the bowl as needed. Refrigerate until needed. 5) In a medium, heavy-bottom saucepan over medium heat, heat the 10 oz [283 g] bag of marshmallows, the remaining ½ cup [120 g] of heavy cream, and the salt, stirring constantly, until the marshmallows have melted, 4 to 5 minutes. Remove from the heat and stir in the vanilla, then let the mixture cool to room temperature. 6) Place the remaining 1 cup [50 g] of marshmallows on an unlined baking sheet and gently toast them with a kitchen torch (if you do not have a kitchen torch, you can place them under the broiler of your oven until they are golden brown). 7) When the marshmallow mixture has cooled, use a spatula to gently fold the chilled whipped cream mixture into the marshmallow mixture until it is completely incorporated. Stir in the toasted marshmallows. Pour the mixture into the prepared crust, then place the baking pan in the refrigerator and chill for at least 4 hours or overnight. 8) FOR THE GLAZE Place the chocolate in a small heatproof bowl. In a small saucepan over low heat, heat the heavy cream until it is simmering and just about to boil. Pour the cream over the chocolate, cover the bowl with plastic wrap, and let sit for 5 minutes. 9) Remove the plastic wrap, add the corn syrup, and stir the chocolate into the cream until completely smooth. 10) Pour the chocolate glaze over the top of the bars, right in the center. Using an offset spatula, cover the whole top with the glaze, carefully smoothing it out as you move it to the edges. Let the glaze set before slicing. 11) When ready to serve, use the parchment sling to gently lift the bars from the pan before cutting into squares. The bars can be stored in the refrigerator, covered, for up to 2 days.

Another classic no-bake recipe, this dessert uses graham crackers to create "cake" layers. I use my pastry cream as a base and add some chocolate to it for a very rich, delicious treat.

Chocolate Éclair Cake

MAKES · 12 LARGE OR
24 SMALL SQUARES

FILLING

5 large egg yolks, at room temperature

1½ cups [300 g] granulated sugar

¼ cup [25 g] Dutch-process cocoa powder

½ teaspoon salt

¼ cup [28 g] cornstarch

1 cup [240 g] whole milk

2½ cups [600 g] heavy cream

2 tablespoons unsalted butter

2 teaspoons pure vanilla extract

8 oz [226 g] semisweet or bittersweet chocolate, melted and cooled

One 14 oz [396 g] box graham crackers

GLAZE

8 oz [226 g] semisweet or bittersweet chocolate, finely chopped

⅔ cup [160 g] heavy cream

2 tablespoons corn syrup

56

1) **FOR THE FILLING** In the bowl of a stand mixer fitted with a paddle, beat the egg yolks on low speed. With the mixer running on low speed, slowly add the granulated sugar, followed by the cocoa powder and salt, then increase the speed to medium. Beat the egg-sugar mixture until very thick and pale yellow, about 5 minutes. Scrape down the sides of the bowl and add the cornstarch, then mix on low speed until combined. 2) In a medium, heavy-bottom saucepan over medium-low heat, warm the milk and 1 cup [240 g] of the heavy cream until just about to simmer. Remove the pan from the heat and pour the mixture into a medium liquid measuring cup with a pour-able spout.

cont'd

3) With the mixer running on low speed, very slowly add the hot milk mixture, mixing until completely combined. Transfer the mixture back to the saucepan and cook over medium-low heat, stirring constantly with a wooden spoon, until the pastry cream becomes very thick and begins to boil, 5 to 7 minutes. Switch to a whisk and whisk the mixture until the pastry cream thickens and is glossy and smooth, 3 to 4 minutes. Remove the pan from the heat and strain the pastry cream through a fine-mesh sieve into a medium bowl. 4) Stir in the butter and vanilla. Stir in the melted chocolate and mix until smooth and combined. Cover with plastic wrap, making sure the wrap sits directly on top of the cream (this will help keep it from forming a skin). Place in the refrigerator until well chilled, 2 to 3 hours. 5) When the chocolate pastry cream has chilled, in the bowl of a stand mixer fitted with a whisk, beat the remaining 1½ cups [360 g] of heavy cream on low speed until small bubbles form, about 30 seconds. Increase the speed to medium and continue beating until the cream is smooth, thick, and nearly doubled in volume, 2 to 3 minutes. Using a spatula, gently fold the whipped cream into the chocolate pastry cream. It will be a little stiff at first, but the cream will incorporate; just keep mixing until it is completely combined.

6) Line the bottom of a 9 by 13 in [23 by 33 cm] baking pan with about a third of the graham crackers in a single layer, breaking up the crackers as needed to fill in any spaces. Top the crackers with half of the chocolate filling. Add another layer of graham crackers over the filling, then top with the remaining chocolate filling. Cover the top of the filling with the remaining third of the graham crackers. Chill the éclair for at least 6 hours and up to overnight. 7) FOR THE GLAZE Place the semisweet chocolate in a small heatproof bowl. In a small saucepan over low heat, heat the heavy cream until it is simmering and just about to boil. Pour the cream over the chocolate, cover the bowl with plastic wrap, and let sit for 5 minutes. 8) Remove the plastic wrap, add the corn syrup, and stir the chocolate into the cream until completely smooth. 9) Pour the glaze over the top of the graham cracker layer, right in the center. Using an offset spatula, cover the whole top with the glaze, carefully smoothing it out as you move it to the edges. Place the pan back in the refrigerator and let the éclair chill for 1 hour. When ready to serve, cut into squares. Store the bars in the refrigerator, covered, for up to 2 days.

I love a good chocolate bark: it's simple but classy, and can be dressed up or down in so many ways. This version uses white chocolate and freeze-dried raspberry powder to make a quick, tasty treat.

White Chocolate Raspberry Squares

MAKES · ABOUT
48 PIECES

18 oz [510 g] semisweet chocolate, finely chopped

1 lb [455 g] white chocolate, finely chopped

⅓ cup [80 g] heavy cream

1 to 2 tablespoons freeze-dried raspberry powder (see page 16)

2 tablespoons raspberry vodka

57

1) Grease a 9 by 13 in [23 by 33 cm] baking pan and line with a parchment sling. 2) Place 10 oz [280 g] of the semisweet chocolate in a heatproof bowl and set it over a saucepan of barely simmering water (do not allow the bottom of the bowl to touch the water). Stir occasionally until the chocolate is melted and smooth. Remove the chocolate from the heat, then pour it into the prepared pan. Tip the pan back and forth to spread the chocolate evenly. Chill in the refrigerator until set, about 15 minutes. 3) While the chocolate is setting, in the same bowl you used to melt the chocolate, combine 8 oz [230 g] of the semisweet chocolate, the heavy cream, freeze-dried raspberry powder,

and vodka. Warm over the barely simmering water again, stirring frequently, until the mixture is just melted and smooth. Let the mixture cool until it is room temperature, about 15 minutes. Remove the baking pan from the refrigerator and pour the semisweet chocolate—raspberry mixture over the chilled chocolate in the pan. Use an offset spatula to spread it in an even layer. Chill in the refrigerator until very cold and firm, about 1 hour. 4) In a clean bowl, warm 14 oz [400 g] of the white chocolate over barely simmering water until the chocolate is smooth. Remove from the heat and add the remaining 2 oz [57 g] of white chocolate to the warm chocolate and stir until completely melted.

Working quickly, pour the chocolate over the firm semisweet chocolate–raspberry layer, using a clean spatula to spread it to cover. Chill in the refrigerator just until firm, about 20 minutes. 5) Carefully remove the chocolate bark using the parchment sling and transfer to a cutting board. Cut the bark crosswise into six strips, then cut the strips into small squares or triangles. 6) Store the bark in an airtight container, layering sheets of wax or parchment paper between the layers so they don't stick to one another. The bark can be stored in the refrigerator, covered, for up to 1 week.

CHAPTER 5

For a Crowd

"Catherine **hoped** at least to pass **uncensured through the crowd.** As for admiration, it was always **very welcome** when it came, but **she did not depend on it.**"

—Jane Austen, *Northanger Abbey*

I've made these blondies a million times, for every possible occasion. When we made them at the Blue Heron Coffeehouse, they were a customer favorite immediately, and forever a bakery case staple. While many of my afternoons in college were highlighted by this coffee bar, they have also made appearances throughout my adult life: birthdays, funerals, baby showers, after-school snacks, or just because. They bake up thin, full of chocolate and espresso, and they are truly perfect.

Coffee Blondies

MAKES · 24 LARGE
OR 48 SMALL SQUARES

1½ cups [3 sticks or 339 g] unsalted butter

3 cups [600 g] brown sugar

1½ teaspoons salt

¼ cup [60 g] espresso or strong, freshly brewed coffee

3 tablespoons pure vanilla extract

3 large eggs, at room temperature

1 tablespoon baking powder

3 cups [420 g] all-purpose flour

1½ cups [170 g] pecan halves, toasted and chopped

1½ cups [255 g] semisweet chocolate chips

1) Position an oven rack in the middle of the oven and preheat the oven to 350°F [180°C]. Grease a sheet pan. 2) In a large saucepan over medium heat, melt the butter, brown sugar, and salt together until the sugar and salt have dissolved and the butter is completely melted. Remove from the heat, then stir in the espresso and vanilla. Let the mixture cool to room temperature. Add the eggs and baking powder and whisk until combined. Add the flour and stir until just combined. Add the pecans and chocolate chips and stir gently. 3) Transfer the mixture to the prepared pan and use an offset spatula to smooth it into an even layer. 4) Bake for 18 to 24 minutes, until the blondies are set on the edges, the top is golden brown and just beginning to form cracks, and a wooden skewer or toothpick inserted into the blondies comes out with just a couple of crumbs. Transfer the pan to a wire rack and let cool completely. Cut into squares and serve. The blondies can be stored in an airtight container at room temperature for up to 2 days.

Is it wise to make brownies even more decadent than they already are?
When you're adding marshmallows and peanuts, and then ganache
and more chocolate, yes, yes, yes.

Rocky Road Brownies

MAKES · 24 LARGE OR
48 SMALL SQUARES

BROWNIES

6 large eggs, at room temperature

2 cups [400 g] granulated sugar

¾ cup [150 g] brown sugar

¾ cup [170 g] vegetable or canola oil

2 teaspoons pure vanilla extract

1¼ teaspoons salt

1½ teaspoons baking powder

10 oz [283 g] semisweet or bittersweet chocolate, chopped

12 tablespoons [1½ sticks or 170 g] unsalted butter

⅓ cup [33 g] Dutch-process cocoa powder

2 cups [284 g] all-purpose flour

2 cups [100 g] mini marshmallows

1 cup [180 g] semisweet chocolate chips

TOPPING

8 oz [226 g] semisweet or bittersweet chocolate

1 cup [180 g] heavy cream

1 cup [180 g] semisweet chocolate chips

1 cup [140 g] roasted peanuts

1) Position an oven rack in the middle of the oven and preheat the oven to 350°F [180°C]. Grease a sheet pan. 2) **FOR THE BROWNIES** In a large bowl, whisk together the eggs, granulated and brown sugars, oil, vanilla, salt, and baking powder. 3) In a medium, heavy-bottom saucepan over low heat, melt the semisweet chocolate and butter, stirring frequently to prevent scorching. Continue cooking until the mixture is smooth. Remove from the heat and add the cocoa powder and whisk until completely combined. 4) Add the chocolate mixture to the sugar-egg mixture and whisk until smooth. Add the flour and stir with a spatula until just combined.

59

5) Pour the batter into the prepared pan and bake for 18 to 24 minutes, until the sides of the brownies have set, the top is starting to crackle and look glossy, and a wooden skewer or toothpick inserted into the center comes out with crumbs. The batter on the toothpick should not be wet but should have a good amount of crumbs clinging to it. 6) Transfer the pan to a wire rack. Sprinkle the mini marshmallows and chocolate chips over the warm brownies and gently press them in so they adhere. 7) FOR THE TOPPING While the brownies bake, place the semisweet chocolate in a small heatproof bowl. In a small saucepan over medium heat, heat the heavy cream until it is simmering and just about to boil. Pour the cream over the chocolate, cover the bowl with plastic wrap, and let it sit for 5 minutes. Remove the plastic wrap and whisk until completely smooth. 8) Pour the chocolate ganache evenly over the middle section of the warm brownies, then use an offset spatula to spread it over the top. It will be a little tricky due to the marshmallow bumps, but go slow and start in the center, working toward the edges. Sprinkle the top with the chocolate chips and peanuts. Let the brownies cool completely, then cut into squares and serve. The brownies can be stored in the refrigerator, covered, for up to 3 days.

I have a thing for cream-cheese-and-jam-filled, streusel-topped coffee cakes.
They are in my top five of favorite comforting eats, especially when freshly
baked and just warm to the touch. This version is made in a half sheet pan, which
provides the perfect cake-to-filling-to-streusel ratio, in my opinion.

Raspberry Almond Coffee Cake Squares

MAKES · 24 LARGE OR
48 SMALL SQUARES

CAKE

1 cup [240 g] sour cream,
at room temperature

⅓ cup [80 g] buttermilk,
at room temperature

1 large egg, at room
temperature

1 teaspoon pure vanilla
extract

1 teaspoon pure almond
extract, or to taste

3½ cups [497 g]
all-purpose flour

1½ cups [300 g]
granulated sugar

1 cup [2 sticks or 227 g]
unsalted butter, cut into
1 in [2.5 cm] pieces, at
room temperature

1¾ cups [175 g] sliced
almonds

¾ teaspoon baking
powder

¾ teaspoon baking soda

¾ teaspoon salt

1½ cups [336 g]
raspberry jam

FILLING

12 oz [340 g] cream
cheese, at room
temperature

⅓ cup [65 g] granulated
sugar

1 large egg, at room
temperature

1) FOR THE CAKE Position an oven rack
in the middle of the oven and preheat the
oven to 350°F [180°C]. Grease a sheet pan.
2) In a large bowl or liquid measuring cup,
whisk together the sour cream, buttermilk,
egg, vanilla, and almond extract. 3) In the
bowl of a stand mixer fitted with a paddle,
combine the flour and granulated sugar on
low speed. Add the butter, one piece at a
time, beating until the mixture resembles
coarse sand. Transfer 1½ cups [200 g] of
the mixture to a medium bowl and toss with
the sliced almonds. Set aside. 4) With the
mixer running on low speed, beat in the
baking powder, baking soda, and salt. Add
the wet ingredients and mix until incorporated, about 30 seconds. Remove the bowl
from the mixer. Scrape down the sides
of the bowl and use a spatula to mix the

batter a few more times. Pour the batter into the prepared pan and use an offset spatula to smooth the top. Spread the jam evenly over the cake batter. 5) **FOR THE FILLING** In the same stand mixer bowl, beat together the cream cheese and granulated sugar on low speed until smooth and creamy. Add the egg and mix until incorporated, stopping to scrape down the sides of the bowl as needed. Pour the filling over the jam and smooth the top with an offset spatula. Sprinkle the reserved almond mixture over the cream cheese and gently pat it into an even layer over the batter. Tap the pan gently on the counter twice to get rid of any air bubbles. 6) Bake for 26 to 35 minutes, rotating the pan halfway through baking, until the cake is golden brown and a wooden skewer or toothpick inserted into the center comes out with a few crumbs. Transfer the pan to a wire rack and let cool until barely warm or at room temperature. Cut the cake into squares and serve. Alternatively, the cake can be covered in plastic wrap after cooling and stored in the refrigerator overnight.

This recipe for cheesecake bars is a personal favorite; it's easy to assemble and so delicious. These bars bake up thin but still have a tangy, creamy filling. I love raspberry jam swirled throughout, but you could use your favorite flavor of jam instead.

Raspberry Mascarpone Cheesecake Tart

MAKES · 24 LARGE OR 48 SMALL SQUARES

CRUST

2½ cups [250 g] graham cracker crumbs

1 cup [142 g] all-purpose flour

¼ cup [50 g] granulated sugar

¼ teaspoon salt

8 tablespoons [113 g] unsalted butter, melted and cooled

CREAM CHEESE FILLING

20 oz [567 g] cream cheese, at room temperature

1 cup [240 g] mascarpone cheese, at room temperature

1 cup [200 g] granulated sugar

¼ teaspoon salt

1 large egg, at room temperature

1 teaspoon lemon juice

1 teaspoon pure vanilla extract

1 cup [224 g] store-bought raspberry jam

1) FOR THE CRUST Position an oven rack in the middle of the oven and preheat the oven to 325°F [165°C]. Grease a sheet pan. 2) In a large bowl, whisk together the graham cracker crumbs, flour, granulated sugar, and salt. Add the melted butter and stir to combine. 3) Pat the dough into the prepared pan and bake for 12 minutes. Transfer the pan to a wire rack and let the crust cool while you prepare the filling. 4) FOR THE CREAM CHEESE FILLING In the bowl of a stand mixer fitted with a paddle, beat the cream cheese, mascarpone, granulated sugar, and salt on medium speed until smooth. Scrape down the sides of the bowl and add the egg, lemon juice, and vanilla, mixing until completely combined. 5) Pour the filling over the prepared crust and use an offset spatula to spread it evenly. Dollop the raspberry jam over the

top of the filling, then use the tip of a butter knife to swirl the jam into the cream cheese batter, being careful not to cut into the crust. Bang the bottom of the pan on the counter a few times to help get rid of any air bubbles.

6) Bake until the sides are slightly puffed and the center doesn't jiggle when shaken, 25 to 30 minutes. Remove the pan from the oven and transfer to a wire rack and let cool. Once completely cool, move to the refrigerator and chill for at least 4 hours or overnight before slicing. Store the bars in an airtight container in the refrigerator for up to 2 days.

61

These squares faintly remind me of a certain soft, fruit-filled breakfast bar I love but seldom buy for myself. Using blueberries makes assembly an easy affair, and I enjoy these on the second day, when they have had time to soften and develop more flavor.

MAKES · 24 LARGE OR
48 SMALL SQUARES

Blueberry Crumble Bars

FILLING

¾ cup [150 g] granulated sugar

¼ cup [28 g] cornstarch

1 teaspoon ground cinnamon

½ teaspoon salt

8 cups [1.2 kg] blueberries, fresh or frozen

1 tablespoon lemon juice

CRUST

5 cups [710 g] all-purpose flour

1 cup [90 g] rolled oats

1 cup [200 g] granulated sugar

1 cup [200 g] brown sugar

2 teaspoons baking powder

1 teaspoon salt

2 cups [4 sticks or 455 g] unsalted butter, at room temperature

1) Position an oven rack in the middle of the oven and preheat the oven to 350°F [180°C]. Grease a sheet pan. 2) FOR THE FILLING In a small bowl, whisk together the granulated sugar, cornstarch, cinnamon, and salt. 3) In a large bowl, mix together the berries and lemon juice. Pour the sugar mixture over the berries and stir gently with a spatula to evenly combine. Set aside. 4) FOR THE CRUST In the bowl of a stand mixer fitted with a paddle, mix the flour, oats, granulated and brown sugars, baking powder, and salt on low speed to combine. Add the butter and mix on low speed until the mixture resembles coarse sand. Press about one-third of the mixture into the bottom of the prepared pan. Use a measuring cup to press it down into a nice, tight layer. Bake for 15 minutes.

5) Remove the pan from the oven, spread the filling over the crust, and sprinkle the remaining flour-oat mixture evenly over the top, pressing it gently into the blueberry filling in an even layer. 6) Bake for 45 to 60 minutes, until the crumbly top is light golden brown and the fruit juices have started to bubble. Transfer the pan to a wire rack and let cool completely. Place the pan in the refrigerator and let the bars chill for 4 to 6 hours. Cut the bars into squares and serve. The bars can be served cold or at room temperature and will keep in the refrigerator, covered, for up to 3 days.

I have these bars on my website but felt I also must include them here because they are a perfect autumn treat for large gatherings. This recipe is similar to most pumpkin bar or cake recipes found in old cookbooks, but I've tweaked it over the years to include some maple syrup and a little more salt. I like how these bars bake up thin, and I find they have the perfect cake-to-icing ratio. I also love them cold, straight from the fridge.

Pumpkin Bars

MAKES · 24 LARGE OR
48 SMALL SQUARES

15 ounces [425 g] unsweetened pumpkin purée

4 large eggs, at room temperature

1 cup [240 g] vegetable or canola oil

¾ cup [150 g] granulated sugar

¾ cup [150 g] brown sugar

3 tablespoons maple syrup

2 teaspoons baking powder

2 teaspoons ground cinnamon

1 teaspoon baking soda

1 teaspoon pure vanilla extract

1 teaspoon salt

¾ teaspoon ground ginger

½ teaspoon freshly grated nutmeg

Pinch of ground cloves

2 cups [284 g] all-purpose flour

2 recipes Cream Cheese Buttercream (page 250)

1) Position an oven rack in the middle of the oven and preheat the oven to 350°F [180°C]. Grease a sheet pan. 2) In a large bowl, whisk together the pumpkin, eggs, oil, granulated and brown sugars, maple syrup, baking powder, cinnamon, baking soda, vanilla, salt, ginger, nutmeg, and cloves until combined. Add the flour and use a spatula to combine it with the batter, making sure to check for any flour pockets in the batter. Use a whisk to eliminate any remaining flour lumps in the dough, about 10 seconds. Spread the batter evenly in the prepared pan, using an offset spatula to smooth the top. 3) Bake the bars until they are set and a wooden skewer or toothpick inserted into the center comes out clean, 15 to 20 minutes. Transfer the pan to a wire rack and let cool completely. Transfer the pan to the

refrigerator and let chill for 2 hours. 4) Dollop the buttercream in thirds across the surface of the chilled bars, then use an offset spatula to spread it evenly over the entire surface. Place the pan in the refrigerator for at least 1 hour or overnight (the bars will slice best if chilled). Cut the bars into squares and serve. The bars can be stored in the refrigerator, covered, for 3 days.

I didn't grow up eating handheld pies from that famous fast-food restaurant, but my husband and father-in-law did, and the nostalgia that hit them when trying a piece of this slab pie was reason enough to include it in this chapter. These bars are made for a crowd and bake up thin in a half sheet pan, but there is still a flaky crust, plenty of cherry flavor, and a dreamy icing to top things off. My time-saving trick is to use store-bought frozen cherries; there is no pitting required, and cooking down the thawed juices with cornstarch makes less risk of a leaky pie.

Cherry Pie Bars

MAKES · 24 LARGE OR
48 SMALL SQUARES

CRUST

¾ cup [180 g] milk, plus more as needed

¼ cup [60 g] Crème Fraîche (page 278) or store-bought

3 large egg yolks

5 cups [710 g] all-purpose flour, plus more for dusting

⅓ cup [65 g] granulated sugar

2 teaspoons salt

2 cups [4 sticks or 455 g] unsalted butter, cut into 30 pieces

Egg wash (see page 16)

CHERRY FILLING

12 cups [1.4 kg] sweet cherries, or a combination of sweet and tart cherries (see note, page 184), frozen, thawed, and chopped into bite-size pieces

⅔ cup [130 g] granulated sugar

5 tablespoons [35 g] cornstarch

1 teaspoon lemon juice

½ teaspoon ground cinnamon

½ teaspoon salt

3 tablespoons unsalted butter, melted

1 tablespoon kirsch (optional)

2 teaspoons pure vanilla extract

ICING

3 tablespoons milk

2 tablespoons unsalted butter, melted

1 teaspoon pure vanilla extract

1 teaspoon lemon juice

¼ teaspoon salt

1½ to 2 cups [180 to 240 g] confectioners' sugar

64

1) **FOR THE CRUST** In a small bowl or liquid measuring cup, combine the milk, crème fraîche, and egg yolks. 2) In the bowl of a stand mixer fitted with a paddle, mix the flour, granulated sugar, and salt on low speed until combined. Add half of the chilled butter and mix on low speed until the butter is just starting to break down, about 1 minute. Add the rest of the butter and continue mixing until the butter is broken down in various sizes (some butter will be incorporated into the dough, some will be a bit large, but most should be about the size of small peas). Stop the mixer and use your hands to check for any dry patches of dough on the bottom of the bowl; incorporate the dry flour as best you can. With the mixer running on low speed, slowly add the milk-egg mixture and mix until the dough starts to come together. If the dough is having trouble coming together, add 1 or 2 more tablespoons of milk. 3) Divide the dough in half, place each piece on a separate piece of plastic wrap, and flatten each slightly into a square. Wrap in the plastic wrap and refrigerate until cool but still soft, about 45 minutes.

cont'd

4) On a lightly floured work surface, roll one square of the dough into a 12 by 16 in [30.5 by 40.5 cm] rectangle. Transfer the dough to a sheet pan and gently pat it into the bottom and up the sides of the pan. Roll out the second piece of dough into a 12 by 16 [30.5 by 40.5 cm] rectangle and place it on a sheet pan lined with parchment paper. Transfer both sheet pans to the refrigerator. 5) FOR THE FILLING Strain the cherry juice from the thawed cherries and reserve the juice; you will have about 1¾ cups [420 g] of juice (a little more or less is just fine). Place the cherries into the large bowl. 6) In a large saucepan, combine the reserved cherry juice, granulated sugar, cornstarch, lemon juice, cinnamon, and salt. Cook over medium heat until thick and translucent, whisking constantly, 3 to 5 minutes. The mixture will go from cloudy and pale to shiny and bright. Remove from the heat and add the butter, kirsch (if using), and vanilla and whisk to combine. 7) Pour the juice mixture over the cherries and stir to combine. Let sit for 5 minutes. 8) Fill the prepared pie shell with the cherry mixture and smooth the top. Remove the rolled-out dough from the second sheet pan and gently cut a few steam vents into the dough. Place the dough over the top of the cherry mixture. The pastry on the bottom and the top of the pan will just be touching, and you can press them together and then crimp the edges with the tines of a fork. Chill the pan in the freezer for 20 minutes while the oven preheats (you can also place the pan in the refrigerator for 40 minutes if it will not fit in your freezer). 9) Position an oven rack in the lowest position and preheat the oven to 400°F [200°C]. Place a sheet pan upside down on the oven rack (the preheated sheet pan helps crisp the bottom of the pie crust). 10) When ready to bake, brush the top of the pie with the egg wash. Place the filled pie pan on the preheated sheet pan and bake for 40 to 55 minutes, until the crust is golden brown and the juices are bubbling. 11) Transfer the pan to a wire rack and let cool completely. 12) FOR THE ICING In a small bowl, combine the milk, melted butter, vanilla, lemon juice, and salt until smooth. Add 1½ cups [180 g] of the confectioners' sugar and mix until smooth. If the mixture is too thin, add more confectioners' sugar until the desired consistency is reached. 13) Once the bars are cool, top them with the icing. Let the icing set, then cut into squares and serve. The bars are best eaten the same day they are made but can be refrigerated in an airtight container for up to 2 days.

NOTE For a little flavor complexity, swap out some of the sweet cherries for tart. I like to use 2 cups [240 g] tart cherries to help balance the sweetness.

I've been making this cake for over a decade now, and it is always a crowd favorite. There is something about the sweet, dense, yellow cake layer, cream cheese–whipped cream, and fresh berries that hits the spot on a warm summer day. My father-in-law shares his birthday with the Fourth of July, and this is his request every year for a birthday cake.

MAKES · 24 LARGE OR
48 SMALL SQUARES

Strawberry Shortcake Cake

CAKE

3 large eggs, at room temperature

2 large egg yolks, at room temperature

½ cup [120 g] Crème Fraîche (page 278) or sour cream, at room temperature

½ cup [120 g] whole milk, at room temperature

1 tablespoon pure vanilla extract

2 cups [284 g] all-purpose flour

1½ cups [300 g] granulated sugar

¾ teaspoon baking powder

¾ teaspoon baking soda

¾ teaspoon salt

1 cup [2 sticks or 227 g] unsalted butter, cut into 1 in [2.5 cm] pieces, at room temperature

WHIPPED CREAM TOPPING

8 oz [226 g] cream cheese, at room temperature

1 cup [200 g] granulated sugar

¼ teaspoon salt

2 cups [480 g] heavy cream

1 teaspoon pure vanilla extract

2 lb [900 g] strawberries, give or take, chopped or sliced as desired

cont'd

65

1) FOR THE CAKE Position an oven rack in the middle of the oven and preheat the oven to 350°F [180°C]. Grease a sheet pan. 2) In a medium bowl or liquid measuring cup, whisk together the eggs, egg yolks, crème fraîche, milk, and vanilla. 3) In the bowl of a stand mixer fitted with a paddle, mix together the flour, granulated sugar, baking powder, baking soda, and salt on low speed until combined. With the mixer running on low speed, add the butter one piece at a time, beating until the mixture resembles coarse sand. Slowly add half the wet ingredients. Increase the speed to medium and beat until incorporated, about 30 seconds. With the mixer running on low speed, add the rest of the wet ingredients, mixing until just combined. Increase the speed to medium and beat for 20 seconds (the batter may still look a little lumpy). Scrape down the sides and bottom of the bowl and use a spatula to mix the batter a few more times. 4) Pour the batter into the prepared pan and smooth the top. Tap the pan gently on the counter two or three times to help get rid of any air bubbles. Bake for 15 to 18 minutes, rotating the pan halfway through, until the cake is golden brown and pulls away slightly from the sides, and a wooden skewer or toothpick inserted into the center comes out clean. 5) Transfer the pan to a wire rack and let cool completely. Chill the cake for at least 2 hours before frosting. Alternatively, the cake can be wrapped in plastic in the pan and refrigerated overnight, then frosted.

6) FOR THE WHIPPED CREAM TOPPING In the bowl of a stand mixer fitted with a paddle, beat the cream cheese on low speed until smooth. Add the granulated sugar and salt and beat on low speed until smooth and light, about 3 minutes. Scrape down the sides of the bowl and fit the mixer with a whisk. With the mixer running on low speed, slowly add the heavy cream, whisking until fully combined. Increase the speed to medium and beat until soft peaks form, stopping to scrape down the sides of the bowl as necessary, 4 to 6 minutes. Add the vanilla and mix on low speed until just combined. 7) Dollop the topping over the chilled bars and use an offset spatula to spread it evenly over the entire surface. Decorate with the chopped or sliced strawberries as desired. Cut the cake into squares and serve. The cake can be stored in an airtight container in the refrigerator for 2 days.

VARIATION

• **Flag Cake:** *Use blueberries and strawberries to decorate the top of the frosted cake to resemble the American flag.*

This treat is inspired by Cathy Barrow's recipe for Good Morning Cheese Danish Slab from her wonderful book *Pie Squared*. I have a version in *100 Morning Treats* that uses Danish dough, but I've swapped it out here for my Cheater Croissant Dough (page 264), which results in a delicious, flaky crust that feeds even more friends.

Lemon Streusel Squares

MAKES · 20 SQUARES

All-purpose flour, for dusting

½ recipe Cheater Croissant Dough (page 264)

Egg wash (see page 16)

1¼ cups [400 g] Lemon Curd (page 282)

1½ cups [210 g] Streusel, page 287

Confectioners' sugar, for dusting (optional)

1) On a generously floured work surface, roll out the dough to a 12 by 16 in [30.5 by 40.5 cm] rectangle and place on a parchment-lined sheet pan. 2) With a sharp knife or bench scraper, score the pastry almost all the way through the dough to mark off 20 equal squares. Loosely cover the dough with lightly greased plastic wrap and let the dough rise at room temperature until puffed, 1 to 1½ hours. 3) Position an oven rack in the middle of the oven and preheat the oven to 350°F [180°C]. 4) Brush the dough with the egg wash. Use a small scoop or two spoons to dollop about 1 tablespoon of the lemon curd on top of each pastry square. Sprinkle the top of the pastry with the streusel, avoiding the lemon curd dollops. 5) Bake for 18 to 24 minutes, rotating the pan halfway through, until the pastry is golden brown. Transfer the pan to a wire rack and let cool for a few minutes. Dust with the confectioners' sugar (if using), then slice through the pre-cut lines and serve just warm to the touch. This pastry is best eaten the same day it is made.

66

On a whim one day, I added pretzels to my shortbread; the salty pretzels balance the sugar in each bite and lend more flavor and texture to the shortbread base.

MAKES · 36 SERVINGS

Pretzel Shortbread Fingers

2 large egg yolks, at room temperature

1 tablespoon pure vanilla extract

3½ cups [500 g] all-purpose flour

1 cup [100 g] pretzels

1 cup [200 g] granulated sugar, plus more for sprinkling

1 cup [120 g] confectioners' sugar

1 teaspoon salt

2 cups [4 sticks or 455 g] unsalted butter, at room temperature

1) Position an oven rack in the middle of the oven and preheat the oven to 400°F [200°C]. Grease a sheet pan. **2)** In a small liquid measuring cup or bowl, use a fork to combine the egg yolks and vanilla. **3)** In the bowl of a food processor fitted with a blade, pulse the flour, pretzels, granulated and confectioners' sugars, and salt together until the pretzels are broken down, 10 one-second pulses. Scatter the butter over the top of the flour mixture and pulse until the mixture looks like wet sand, 10 to 15 one-second pulses. Pour the egg yolk mixture over the top of the flour mixture and pulse until the dough is smooth and starts to pull away from the sides of the food processor, about 10 more one-second pulses. **4)** Scrape the dough out of the processor and into the prepared pan. Pat the dough into an even layer, smoothing the top with the bottom of a measuring cup. Score the

67

shortbread into thirty-six 1½ by 4 in [4 by 10 cm] pieces with a knife, cutting through the dough, and use the tines of a fork or wooden skewer to poke holes in each piece if desired (these are purely for decoration). Sprinkle the top of the shortbread generously with granulated sugar.

5) Place the shortbread in the oven and lower the temperature to 300°F [150°C]. Bake until the shortbread is pale golden and firm to the touch, 45 minutes to 1 hour. Transfer the pan to a wire rack. Sprinkle with more granulated sugar, if desired, and let the shortbread cool at room temperature for several hours. Cut the shortbread at the scored marks. The short-bread can be stored in an airtight container at room temperature for up to 4 days.

NOTE If you don't have a big enough food processor, you can make this shortbread the opposite way in a stand mixer: Crush the pretzels until they are very small crumbs. Beat the butter on low speed until creamy. Add the granu-lated and confectioners' sugars and mix together on medium speed until light and fluffy, 3 to 4 minutes. Scrape down the sides of the bowl and add the egg yolks, vanilla, and salt, mixing on low speed until combined. Add the flour and pret-zel crumbs and mix on low speed until combined. Shape and bake as directed.

Rhubarb and caramel are delicious paired together, and I give a nod to the rhubarb crisp that always graces church potlucks by topping these bars with a heavy layer of streusel. A giant scoop of No-Churn Ice Cream (page 283) is the perfect addition to the warm bars.

Caramel Rhubarb Shortbread Bars

MAKES · 24 LARGE OR 48 SMALL SQUARES

SHORTBREAD CRUST

5½ cups [781 g] all-purpose flour

2 cups [400 g] granulated sugar

½ cup [50 g] almond flour

1 teaspoon baking powder

1 teaspoon salt

¾ teaspoon ground cinnamon

1 large egg, at room temperature

2 cups [4 sticks or 455 g] unsalted butter, at room temperature, cut into 1 in [2.5 cm] pieces

FILLING

½ cup [120 g] apple cider

¼ cup [28 g] cornstarch

7 cups [908 g] rhubarb, fresh or frozen, cut into 1 in [2.5 cm] pieces

1 recipe Caramel (page 276)

1) Position an oven rack in the middle of the oven and preheat the oven to 350°F [180°C]. Grease a sheet pan. 2) **FOR THE SHORTBREAD CRUST** In the bowl of a stand mixer fitted with a paddle, mix together the all-purpose flour, granulated sugar, almond flour, baking powder, salt, and cinnamon on low speed to combine. Add the egg and mix until incorporated, then add the butter and mix on low speed until the mixture resembles coarse sand. 3) Transfer a little less than half of the mixture into the bottom of the prepared pan and press it into the pan so it is a tight, even layer. Bake for 10 minutes. 4) **FOR THE FILLING** While the crust is baking, in a medium saucepan over medium heat, cook the apple cider and cornstarch, stirring constantly, until the cornstarch is dissolved and the mixture

68

has thickened and is glossy, 3 to 4 minutes. 5) Place the rhubarb in a large bowl and pour the thickened cornstarch mixture over it, then use a spatula to stir until evenly coated. Pour the caramel over the rhubarb and stir to evenly coat again. 6) Remove the pan from the oven and spread the filling over the crust in an even layer. Cover the filling with the remaining crust mixture, pressing it into the filling in an even layer. 7) Bake for 40 to 55 minutes, until the top is light golden brown and the fruit juices have started to bubble. Transfer the pan to a wire rack and let cool to room temperature before slicing. The bars can be served cold or at room temperature and will keep in the refrigerator in an airtight container for 3 days.

A nod to my favorite childhood lunch, but in much better form (cake). I spent quite a bit of time getting this recipe just right; I found adding ground peanuts to the batter helped keep the cake moist, and spreading the jam over the warm cake helped lock in the raspberry flavor. Candied peanuts added needed crunch and ramp up the peanut butter flavor.

Peanut Butter and Jelly Cake

MAKES · 24 LARGE OR 48 SMALL SQUARES

1 cup [240 g] water

¾ cup [162 g] creamy peanut butter

8 tablespoons [1 stick or 113 g] unsalted butter

1½ cups [300 g] granulated sugar

½ cup [100 g] brown sugar

1 teaspoon salt

1 tablespoon pure vanilla extract

⅓ cup [50 g] roasted peanuts, salted or lightly salted

½ cup [120 g] buttermilk, at room temperature

3 large eggs, at room temperature

¼ cup [56 g] vegetable or canola oil

1 teaspoon baking powder

1 teaspoon baking soda

1¾ cups [250 g] all-purpose flour

2 cups [448 g] raspberry jam

1 recipe Peanut Butter Buttercream (page 253)

1 recipe Candied Nuts, peanut variation (page 284)

1) **FOR THE CAKE** Position an oven rack in the middle of the oven and preheat the oven to 350°F [180°C]. Grease a sheet pan. 2) In a large saucepan, combine the water, peanut butter, and butter. Cook over medium heat, whisking often, until the butter has melted and the mixture is combined. Add the granulated and brown sugars and salt and mix until the sugars are dissolved and combined, about 1 minute. Remove from the heat and add the vanilla, then let the mixture cool to room temperature. 3) In the bowl of a food processor fitted with a blade, process the peanuts until they are completely broken down.

69

4) Add the processed peanuts, buttermilk, eggs, oil, baking powder, and baking soda to the cooled mixture and whisk to combine. Stir in the flour with a spatula and mix until combined. Pour the batter into the prepared pan and tap it gently on the counter twice to release any air bubbles. 5) Bake the cake for 18 to 25 minutes, until a wooden skewer or toothpick inserted into the center comes out clean. Move the pan to a wire rack and spread the jam in an even layer over the warm cake. Let the cake cool completely before frosting. 6) Once the cake is cool, spread the peanut butter buttercream over the top, then sprinkle the candied peanuts evenly over the cake. Cut the cake and serve. The cake can be stored in the refrigerator, covered, for up to 2 days.

This is inspired by the famous Texas sheet cake—a large, thin, chocolate cake covered in icing and often pecans. I found that most recipes had a small amount of cocoa in the cake (which just wasn't enough chocolate for me) and the icing was often too sweet. My Midwestern version of the cake needed a good dose of chocolate, then more chocolate in the form of ganache poured over the warm cake. Black walnuts—candied for plenty of sweet-salty crunch—top the whole thing off, as they are native to Minnesota. Now I just need a potluck to bring this beauty to . . .

Minnesota Sheet Cake

MAKES · 24 LARGE OR
48 SMALL SQUARES

CAKE

1 cup [200 g] granulated sugar

1 cup [200 g] brown sugar

8 tablespoons [1 stick or 113 g] unsalted butter, melted

¾ cup [75 g] Dutch-process cocoa powder

½ cup [112 g] vegetable or canola oil

½ cup [120 g] Crème Fraîche (page 278) or sour cream, at room temperature

3 large eggs, at room temperature

2 large egg yolks, at room temperature

2 teaspoons pure vanilla extract

1 teaspoon salt

1 teaspoon baking soda

½ teaspoon baking powder

2 cups [284 g] all-purpose flour

¾ cup [180 g] strong, freshly brewed coffee, hot

ASSEMBLY

1 recipe Ganache (page 257), half sheet pan variation

2 cups [260 g] Candied Nuts (page 284), black walnut or pecan variation

1) FOR THE CAKE Position an oven rack in the middle of the oven and preheat the oven to 350°F [180°C]. Grease a sheet pan. 2) In a large bowl, whisk together the granulated and brown sugars, melted butter, cocoa powder, oil, crème fraîche, eggs, egg yolks, vanilla, salt, baking soda, and baking powder. Add the flour and use a spatula to combine it into the batter. Slowly pour the hot coffee into the batter and mix until just combined. Pour the batter into the prepared pan and use an offset spatula to smooth the top. 3) Bake for 18 to 24 minutes, until a wooden skewer or toothpick inserted into the center comes out with the tiniest bit of crumb. Transfer the pan to a wire rack and let cool for 5 minutes. 4) TO ASSEMBLE Pour the ganache over the warm cake, using an offset spatula to smooth it

over the top. Sprinkle the ganache with the candied black walnuts. Let sit until the cake is cooled to room temperature. Chill, if desired, then cut into squares and serve. The cake can be stored in the refrigerator, covered, for up to 3 days.

70

CHAPTER 6

Weekend Projects

"It was afternoon tea, with tea foods spread out,

Like in the books, except that it was coffee."

—Alberto Rios, "Coffee in the Afternoon"

Morning buns are the gold standard of breakfast pastries, with their sweet, swirled cinnamon-orange centers wrapped in a flaky, buttery blanket. An afternoon cake adaption of this favorite breakfast treat seemed like an important contribution to both the cake genre and afternoons in general. If you are looking to sneak in that last espresso drink before the afternoon cutoff, this cake is a perfect accompaniment.

Orange-Cinnamon Swirl Cake

MAKES · ONE 9 IN
[23 CM] CAKE

ORANGE-CINNAMON SWIRL

⅓ cup [65 g] granulated sugar

1 tablespoon orange zest

1 tablespoon ground cinnamon

Pinch of salt

CAKE

10 tablespoons [140 g] unsalted butter, melted and cooled

1¼ cups [250 g] granulated sugar

3 large eggs, at room temperature

½ cup [120 g] Crème Fraîche (page 278), at room temperature

¼ cup [60 g] orange juice

2 tablespoons vegetable or canola oil

1 tablespoon triple sec or other orange liqueur

1 teaspoon pure vanilla extract

1 teaspoon baking powder

¾ teaspoon salt

¼ teaspoon baking soda

2 cups [284 g] all-purpose flour

1) FOR THE ORANGE-CINNAMON SWIRL In a small bowl, combine the granulated sugar, orange zest, cinnamon, and salt. Reserve 2 tablespoons for sprinkling on top. **2) FOR THE CAKE** Position an oven rack in the middle of the oven and preheat the oven to 350°F [180°C]. Grease a 9 in [23 cm] square baking pan and line with a parchment sling. **3)** In a large bowl, whisk together the melted butter, granulated sugar, eggs, crème fraîche, orange juice, oil, triple sec, vanilla, baking powder, salt, and baking soda. Add the flour and use a spatula to stir it into the batter. Switch to a whisk and whisk the batter to eliminate any remaining flour lumps, about 10 seconds. Pour half of the batter into the prepared pan and sprinkle the swirl

71

mixture (minus the reserved 2 tablespoons) over the top. Cover with the rest of the batter and use an offset spatula to smooth the top. Use a butter knife to swirl the batter in a figure eight once or twice, then sprinkle with the remaining 2 tablespoons of swirl mixture. Tap the pan gently on the counter twice to help get rid of any air bubbles. 4) Bake for 32 to 40 minutes, rotating the pan halfway through, until the cake

is golden brown and a wooden skewer or tooth-pick inserted into the center comes out clean. Transfer the pan to a wire rack and let cool for 20 minutes. Use the parchment sling to remove the cake from the pan, transfer to the wire rack, and let cool until just warm to the touch. Cut the cake into squares and serve. The cake can be stored in an airtight container at room temperature for up to 3 days.

My cookbook *100 Morning Treats* has a recipe for Maple Bourbon Caramel Rolls, and I loved the maple-caramel flavor so much I decided to incorporate it here as well. The cake is swirled with a cinnamon-sugar filling, and then the caramel is poured over the warm cake, which makes for a tender, tasty bite.

Maple Bourbon Sticky Bun Cake

MAKES • ONE 9 IN [23 CM] CAKE

CINNAMON SWIRL

¼ cup [50 g] granulated sugar

1 tablespoon ground cinnamon

½ teaspoon freshly grated nutmeg

Pinch of cloves

Pinch of salt

CAKE

10 tablespoons [140 g] unsalted butter, melted and cooled

1¼ cups [250 g] granulated sugar

3 large eggs, at room temperature

½ cup [120 g] Crème Fraîche (page 278), at room temperature

¼ cup [60 g] buttermilk

2 tablespoons vegetable or canola oil

1 tablespoon triple sec or other orange liqueur

1 teaspoon pure vanilla extract

1 teaspoon baking powder

¾ teaspoon salt

¼ teaspoon baking soda

2 cups [284 g] all-purpose flour

MAPLE BOURBON CARAMEL

8 tablespoons [1 stick or 113 g] unsalted butter

1 cup [200 g] brown sugar

1 cup [240 g] heavy cream

⅓ cup [107 g] maple syrup

½ teaspoon salt

2 tablespoons bourbon

1 teaspoon pure vanilla extract

¾ cup [90 g] pecan halves, toasted and chopped

cont'd

72

1) FOR THE CINNAMON SWIRL In a small bowl, combine the granulated sugar, cinnamon, nutmeg, cloves, and salt. Set aside. 2) FOR THE CAKE Position an oven rack in the middle of the oven and preheat the oven to 350°F [180°C]. Grease a 9 in [23 cm] square baking pan and line with a parchment sling. 3) In a large bowl, whisk together the melted butter, granulated sugar, eggs, crème fraîche, buttermilk, oil, triple sec, vanilla, baking powder, salt, and baking soda. Add the flour and use a spatula to stir it into the batter. Switch to a whisk and whisk the batter to eliminate any remaining flour lumps, about 10 seconds. Pour half of the batter into the pan, then sprinkle the swirl mixture over the top. Cover with the rest of the batter and use an offset spatula to smooth the top. Use a butter knife to swirl the batter in a figure eight once or twice. Tap the pan gently on the counter twice to help get rid of any air bubbles. 4) Bake for 32 to 40 minutes, rotating the pan halfway through, until the cake is golden brown and a wooden skewer or toothpick inserted into the center comes out clean.

5) FOR THE MAPLE BOURBON CARAMEL While the cake is baking, make the caramel: In a large, heavy-bottom saucepan over medium heat, combine the butter, brown sugar, heavy cream, maple syrup, and salt until the butter has melted. Increase the heat to medium-high and cook until the mixture has thickened slightly and registers 235°F [113°C] on an instant-read thermometer, 6 to 8 minutes. Remove from the heat and add the bourbon and vanilla, stirring to incorporate. Stir a few times while waiting for the cake to finish baking. 6) Transfer the cake pan to a wire rack and immediately pour half of the caramel sauce over the cake, then sprinkle the chopped pecans over the caramel. Let the cake sit for 10 to 15 minutes at room temperature. Pour the remaining caramel over the top, covering the cake evenly. Let the cake cool until just warm to the touch, then use the parchment sling to remove the cake from the pan. Cut the cake into squares and serve. The cake can be stored in an airtight container at room temperature for up to 2 days.

The first time I tried frangipane, it was slathered on bostok, a delicious treat made with day-old brioche. It was sophisticated yet comforting, and I fell in love at first bite. I changed things up slightly here: The base is cake instead of leftover bread, the frangipane swirled into the cake is hazelnut instead of almond, and the entire affair is topped with meringue.

Hazelnut Frangipane Cake

MAKES · 12 LARGE OR
24 SMALL SQUARES

10 tablespoons [140 g] unsalted butter, melted and cooled

1¾ cups [350 g] granulated sugar

Scant ¾ cup [175 g] egg whites (from 5 to 6 large eggs), at room temperature

½ cup [120 g] buttermilk, at room temperature

⅓ cup [80 g] Crème Fraîche (page 278) or sour cream, at room temperature

¼ cup [56 g] vegetable or canola oil

1 tablespoon pure vanilla extract

1 tablespoon cornstarch

1 tablespoon baking powder

1 teaspoon salt

2⅓ cups [331 g] all-purpose flour

1 recipe Almond Cream (page 281), hazelnut variation

1 recipe Meringue (page 258)

½ cup [70 g] hazelnuts, skinned and chopped into bite-size pieces

1) Position an oven rack in the middle of the oven and preheat the oven to 350°F [180°C]. Grease a 9 by 13 in [23 by 33 cm] baking pan and line with a parchment sling. 2) In a large bowl, whisk together the melted butter, granulated sugar, egg whites, buttermilk, crème fraîche, oil, vanilla, cornstarch, baking powder, and salt.

cont'd

73

Add the flour and use a spatula to stir it into the batter. Switch to a whisk and whisk the batter to eliminate any remaining flour lumps, about 10 seconds. Pour the batter into the prepared pan. Dollop the hazelnut cream over the cake batter and fold it into the batter gently with a butter knife six or seven times using a figure-eight motion, then use an offset spatula to smooth the top. Tap the pan on the counter twice to get rid of any air bubbles. 3) Make the meringue as directed. Working quickly, spoon the meringue over the cake batter and swirl it into the batter gently with a butter knife six or seven times using a figure-eight motion, then smooth the top. There should still be a visible amount of meringue on the top, which will bake up as a topping. Sprinkle the chopped hazelnuts evenly over the top of the cake.

4) Bake for 45 to 60 minutes, until the top of the meringue is browned and a wooden skewer or toothpick inserted into the center of the cake comes out clean; make sure you are checking the cake portion and not just the meringue. Transfer the pan to a wire rack to cool. Once cooled, remove the cake from the pan using the parchment sling and slice into squares. The bars can be stored in an airtight container at room temperature for up to 3 days.

Sometimes I like to sneak a little piece of chocolate in the late afternoons for a pick-me-up, and sometimes it's a whole piece of cake. This is a riff on the Sunken Chocolate Bread from my first cookbook, baked in a square. I find the flavor of the chocolate is deeper and darker a day or two after the cake has been made, but a slice of this warm is quite a treat. Do what you have to do.

Sunken Chocolate Cake

MAKES · ONE 8 IN
[20 CM] CAKE

6 oz [170 g] semisweet or bittersweet chocolate

1 cup [240 g] strong, freshly brewed coffee, hot

1 cup [2 sticks or 227 g] unsalted butter, at room temperature

1½ cups [300 g] dark brown sugar

¾ teaspoon salt

2 large eggs, at room temperature

2 teaspoons pure vanilla extract

1 teaspoon baking soda

1½ cups [213 g] all-purpose flour

Cocoa powder, for dusting

1) Position an oven rack in the middle of the oven and preheat the oven to 375°F [190°C]. Grease an 8 in [20 cm] springform baking pan and line with a parchment sling. 2) Place the chocolate in a medium bowl. Pour the hot coffee over the chocolate and let sit for 5 minutes. Stir to combine. 3) In the bowl of a stand mixer fitted with a paddle, beat the butter on medium speed until smooth. Add the dark brown sugar and salt and mix on medium speed until light and fluffy, 2 to 3 minutes. Add the eggs and vanilla and beat on medium speed until fully incorporated, stopping to scrape down the sides of the bowl as necessary. Add the baking soda and mix again until combined. Add the flour and mix on low speed until incorporated. With the mixer still on low, slowly add the hot coffee-chocolate mixture

74

and mix until combined. Use a spatula to finish mixing the batter, making sure it is completely combined. 4) Pour the batter into the prepared pan and bake for 25 minutes. Lower the oven temperature to 325°F [170°C] and bake for 15 to 20 more minutes. The loaf will still be moist inside, so a wooden skewer or toothpick inserted into the center won't come out clean. The cake should look moist under the top crust in the cracks that form, and should jiggle just slightly when gently shaken. 5) Transfer the pan to a wire rack and let cool completely. The cake will sink in the middle as it cools. When ready to serve, use the parchment sling to remove the cake from the pan. Dust with cocoa powder. Slice and serve. The cake can be stored in an airtight container at room temperature for up to 3 days.

NOTE This cake needs a cake pan with a slightly higher side than a normal pan, as it bakes up tall and can spill over the sides without it.

I'm a big fan of figs, probably because of my dad's obsession with Fig Newtons back in the late '80s. They were the only packaged "cookie" to be found in our cupboards, and I spent many afternoons sneaking them, slowly growing to love them over time. In this recipe, I use Thomas Keller's genius way of incorporating flavored butter into his scones; he beats together butter, sugar, cinnamon, and flour, chills the mixture, and distributes it throughout the dough. I added some chopped figs to this mix, and it worked like a charm.

Fig Scones

MAKES · 8 SCONES

FIG BUTTER

2 oz [57 g] dried figs

4 tablespoons [56 g] unsalted butter, at room temperature

1 tablespoon all-purpose flour

1 tablespoon brown sugar

¼ teaspoon ground cinnamon

SCONES

½ cup [120 g] Crème Fraîche (page 278) or sour cream

1 large egg

1 large egg yolk

1 teaspoon pure vanilla extract

2¼ cups [320 g] all-purpose flour, plus more for dusting

¼ cup [50 g] granulated sugar

1 tablespoon baking powder

½ teaspoon salt

8 tablespoons [1 stick or 113 g] unsalted butter, cold, cut into ½ in [13 mm] pieces

Heavy cream, for brushing

ICING

2 to 4 tablespoons milk or orange juice

2 tablespoons unsalted butter, melted

½ teaspoon pure vanilla extract

Pinch of salt

1½ cups [180 g] confectioners' sugar

cont'd

75

1) **FOR THE FIG BUTTER** In the bowl of a food processor fitted with a blade, process the figs until finely chopped. In a medium bowl, combine the chopped figs, butter, flour, brown sugar, and cinnamon and mix with a spatula until completely combined. Pat the fig butter into a 4 in [10 cm] square and wrap with a piece of plastic wrap, then chill in the refrigerator until very firm. 2) **FOR THE SCONES** Line a sheet pan with parchment paper. In a medium bowl or liquid measuring cup, whisk together the crème fraîche, egg, egg yolk, and vanilla. Set aside. 3) In the bowl of a stand mixer fitted with a paddle, combine the flour, granulated sugar, baking powder, and salt. Add the butter and mix on low speed until the flour-coated pieces are the size of peas. 4) Remove the fig butter from the refrigerator and cut into ½ in [13 mm] cubes. Add them to the bowl and mix on low speed until the cubes just begin to break down and are about half their original size. 5) Remove the bowl from the mixer and use a spatula to fold the wet ingredients into the dry until just combined. Transfer the dough to a lightly floured surface and knead four to six times, until it comes together, adding more flour as necessary if the dough is sticky. Pat the dough gently into a square and use a rolling pin to roll it into a 12 in [30.5 cm] square, dusting with flour as necessary. Fold the dough into thirds, like a business letter. Fold the dough in thirds again by folding in the short ends, making a square. Transfer it to the prepared sheet pan and chill it in the freezer for 10 minutes. 6) Return the dough to the floured surface, roll it again into a 12 in [30.5 cm] square, and fold it in thirds. Turn over the dough so it's seam side down and gently roll out the dough into a 12 by 4 in [30.5 by 10 cm] rectangle. With a sharp knife, cut the dough crosswise into 4 equal rectangles, then cut each rectangle into 2 squares. Transfer the scones to the prepared sheet pan and place in the freezer while the oven is preheating. 7) Position an oven rack in the middle of the oven and preheat the oven to 375°F [190°C]. Stack the sheet pan with the scones on another sheet pan. Brush the tops of the scones with a little heavy cream, making sure it doesn't drip down the sides. Bake for 18 to 25 minutes, rotating the pans halfway through, until the tops and bottoms are light golden brown. 8) **FOR THE ICING** While the scones are baking, make the icing: In a medium bowl, whisk together 2 tablespoons of milk, the melted butter, vanilla, and salt until smooth. Add the confectioners' sugar and mix together, then whisk until well combined and smooth. Add more milk, 1 tablespoon at a time, to thin the icing to your preferred consistency; the icing should be thick but pourable. 9) Transfer the top sheet pan to a wire rack and ice the scones immediately with the back of a spoon or an offset spatula. The scones are best eaten the same day they are made.

NOTE Scones can be cut into circles with a biscuit cutter instead of cut into squares or triangles.

I saw a giant cheesecake brownie cake floating around on Instagram and knew I needed to make my own version in bar form. I use my favorite cheesecake and brownie bases; combined, they make an outrageous dessert with a cookie crust for crunch.

MAKES · 12 LARGE OR
24 SMALL SQUARES

Brownie Cheesecake Bars

CRUST

2 cups [200 g] Chocolate Wafer Cookies (page 270) or store-bought (see page 22)

5 tablespoons [70 g] unsalted butter, melted

CHEESECAKE FILLING

24 oz [678 g] cream cheese, at room temperature

1 cup [200 g] granulated sugar

¼ teaspoon salt

¾ cup [180 g] sour cream, at room temperature

1 tablespoon pure vanilla extract

3 large eggs, at room temperature

BROWNIE FILLING

2 large eggs, at room temperature

¾ cup [150 g] granulated sugar

¼ cup [50 g] brown sugar

¼ cup [56 g] vegetable or canola oil

1 teaspoon pure vanilla extract

½ teaspoon salt

½ teaspoon baking powder

4 oz [113 g] semisweet or bittersweet chocolate

4 tablespoons [56 g] unsalted butter

2 tablespoons Dutch-process cocoa powder

¼ cup [36 g] all-purpose flour

76

cont'd

1) FOR THE CRUST Position an oven rack in the middle of the oven and preheat the oven to 325°F [170°C]. Grease a 9 by 13 in [23 by 33 cm] or 10 in [25 cm] square baking pan and line with a parchment sling. 2) Place the wafers in the bowl of a food processor and process until broken down into fine crumbs. Transfer the crumbs to a medium bowl and pour the melted butter over the top. Use a spatula to stir together until well combined. 3) Press the mixture into the bottom of the prepared pan and bake for 10 minutes. Transfer the pan to a wire rack and let cool. 4) FOR THE CHEESE-CAKE FILLING Wipe out the bowl of the food processor. Add the cream cheese, granulated sugar, and salt and pulse until smooth and creamy, 1 to 2 minutes. Add the sour cream and vanilla and pulse again until smooth. Add the eggs and pulse until the mixture is completely combined. Set aside. 5) FOR THE BROWNIES In a large bowl, whisk together the eggs, granu-lated and brown sugars, oil, vanilla, salt, and baking powder. 6) In a small, heavy-bottom saucepan over low heat, add the semisweet chocolate and butter and melt together, stir-ring frequently to prevent scorching. Continue cooking until the mixture is smooth. Remove from the heat and add the cocoa powder and whisk until completely combined. 7) Add the chocolate mixture to the sugar-egg mixture and whisk until smooth. Add the flour and stir with a spatula until just combined. 8) Pour three-fourths of the brownie batter over the cookie crust and use an offset spatula to smooth the top. Pour the cheesecake mixture over the top of the brownie batter, then dollop the remain-ing brownie batter over the cheesecake. Drag the tip of a butter knife through the batter, avoiding the crust, to create swirls. 9) Bake for 35 to 45 minutes, until the sides have set, the cheesecake filling doesn't jiggle, and a wooden skewer or toothpick inserted into the brownie mixture comes out with a few crumbs. Transfer the pan to a wire rack and let cool completely. Place a piece of parchment over the top of the pan (this helps keep condensation off of the cheesecake) and transfer it to the refrigera-tor. Let chill for at least 6 hours or overnight. 10) When ready to serve, use the parchment sling to gently lift the cheesecake brownies from the pan before cutting into squares. Store in the refrigerator, covered, for up to 2 days.

I made a coconut version of this cake a few years ago while testing recipes for my website. My husband was enamored with the creamy buttercream, chocolate ganache, and chocolate chip cake base, even though he is not a fan of coconut. I made it again for his birthday with a plain vanilla base, and after he asked me to marry him again, I knew I had a perfect cake.

Chocolate Chip Buttermilk Cake

MAKES · 12 LARGE OR 24 SMALL SQUARES

1 cup [240 g] buttermilk, at room temperature

Scant 1 cup [210 g] egg whites (from 6 or 7 large eggs), at room temperature (see note, page 220)

½ cup [120 g] Crème Fraîche (page 278) or sour cream, at room temperature

1 tablespoon pure vanilla extract

2¼ cups [320 g] all-purpose flour

2 cups [400 g] granulated sugar

4 teaspoons baking powder

1 teaspoon salt

1 cup [2 sticks or 227 g] unsalted butter, at room temperature, cut into 1 in [2.5 cm] pieces

¾ cup [120 g] mini semisweet chocolate chips or chopped chocolate

1 recipe Ultra Buttercream (page 249)

1 recipe Ganache (page 257)

Chocolate curls, sprinkles, or chocolate pearls, for decorating (optional)

1) Position an oven rack in the middle of the oven and preheat the oven to 350°F [180°C]. Grease a 9 by 13 in [23 by 33 cm] baking pan and line with a parchment sling. 2) In a medium bowl or liquid measuring cup, whisk together the buttermilk, egg whites, crème fraîche, and vanilla.

cont'd

77

3) In the bowl of a stand mixer fitted with a paddle, combine the flour, granulated sugar, baking powder, and salt. With the mixer running on low speed, add the butter, one piece at a time, beating until the mixture resembles coarse sand. With the mixer still running on low speed, slowly add a little more than half of the wet ingredients. Increase the speed to medium and beat until the ingredients are incorporated, about 30 seconds, With the mixer running on low speed, add the rest of the wet ingredients, mixing until just combined. Increase the speed to medium and beat for 20 seconds (the batter may still look a little lumpy). Scrape down the sides and bottom of the bowl, add the chocolate chips, and use a spatula to mix the batter a few more times. 4) Pour the batter into the prepared pan. Tap the pan gently on the counter twice to help get rid of any air bubbles. Bake for 36 to 45 minutes, rotating the pan halfway through, until the cake is golden brown and a wooden skewer or toothpick inserted into the center comes out with a faint bit of crumbs. 5) Transfer the pan to a wire rack and let cool for 20 minutes, then turn the cake out onto the rack, remove the parchment paper, and let cool completely. Once cool, the cake can be frosted or wrapped in plastic wrap and refrigerated overnight. 6) Spread the buttercream over the top of the cake using an offset spatula. Chill until firm, about 2 hours. 7) Place the cake on a wire rack set over a baking sheet lined with parchment paper. Starting in the center of the cake, pour the ganache in a steady stream and work your way out to the edge. Continue pouring over the edges, until the sides are completely covered. Decorate with chocolate curls, sprinkles, or chocolate pearls (if using). Let the ganache set before slicing into squares and serving. The cake can be stored in an airtight container in the refrigerator for 3 days. Let the cake come to room temperature before slicing and serving.

NOTE Because the egg whites aren't being whipped for volume, store-bought egg whites will work here; just make sure they are 100 percent liquid egg whites.

The first tiramisu cake I ever had was at the Blue Heron Coffeehouse. Colleen had made it for a wedding celebration, and we got to try pieces from the sample cakes she made. I was smitten with the mini chocolate chips nestled in the layers and a hint of marsala wine, and I made Larry photocopy the recipe for me. I found it recently and decided to modernize and simplify it: a single layer of cake, soaked in Kahlúa and coffee, with mascarpone whipped into the cream so it holds in the refrigerator.

Tiramisu Cake

MAKES · 12 LARGE OR 24 SMALL SQUARES

CAKE

1¾ cups [350 g] granulated sugar

Scant ¾ cup [175 g] egg whites (from 5 or 6 large eggs), at room temperature

10 tablespoons [140 g] unsalted butter, melted and cooled

½ cup [120 g] buttermilk, at room temperature

⅓ cup [80 g] Crème Fraîche (page 278) or sour cream, at room temperature

¼ cup [56 g] vegetable or canola oil

1 tablespoon pure vanilla extract

1 tablespoon cornstarch

1 tablespoon baking powder

1 teaspoon salt

2⅓ cups [331 g] all-purpose flour

SOAKING SYRUP

½ cup [120 g] strong, freshly brewed coffee

¼ cup [80 g] Kahlúa

⅓ cup [65 g] granulated sugar

Pinch of salt

MASCARPONE TOPPING

6 oz [170 g] mascarpone cheese

⅓ cup [65 g] granulated sugar

¼ teaspoon salt

1½ cups [360 g] heavy cream

2 tablespoons marsala wine

1 teaspoon pure vanilla extract

Cocoa powder, for dusting

78

cont'd

1) FOR THE CAKE Position an oven rack in the middle of the oven and preheat the oven to 350°F [180°C]. Grease a 9 by 13 in [23 by 33 cm] baking pan and line with a parchment sling. 2) In a large bowl, whisk together the granulated sugar, egg whites, melted butter, buttermilk, crème fraîche, oil, vanilla, cornstarch, baking powder, and salt. Add the flour and use a spatula to combine it into the batter. Whisk to eliminate any remaining flour lumps in the batter, about 10 seconds. Pour the batter into the prepared pan and use an offset spatula to smooth the top. Tap the pan on the counter twice to get rid of any air bubbles. 3) Bake for 24 to 32 minutes, until a wooden skewer or toothpick inserted into the center comes out clean. 4) FOR THE SOAKING SYRUP While the cake is baking, in a small saucepan, combine the coffee, Kahlúa, granulated sugar, and salt. Heat over medium heat until the sugar is dissolved, 3 to 4 minutes. 5) Transfer the cake in the pan to a wire rack. Pour the soaking syrup over the entirety of the cake, using all of the mixture. Let the cake cool completely before frosting.

6) FOR THE MASCARPONE TOPPING In the bowl of a stand mixer fitted with a paddle, beat the mascarpone cheese, granulated sugar, and salt on low speed until smooth and light, about 3 minutes. Scrape down the sides of the bowl and fit the mixer with the whisk. With the mixer running on low speed, slowly add the heavy cream, whisking until fully combined. Increase the speed to medium and beat until soft peaks form, 5 to 6 minutes. Add the marsala and vanilla and mix again on low speed until just combined. 7) Top the cooled cake with the mascarpone topping, using an offset spatula to smooth the top. Dust generously with cocoa powder, then refrigerate the cake for at least 2 hours and up to 24 hours. Cut into squares and serve. The cake can be stored in the refrigerator, covered, for up to 2 days.

NOTE The flavor and texture of this cake intensifies and softens the longer it sits in the refrigerator. I love it the day after assembling, served at room temperature.

Back in my Blue Heron days, we had a group of college students who came in every afternoon for a slice of cheesecake and a giant iced mocha; one of the women would order two slices cut into one giant triangle, and I'll never forget how her eyes would light up when I handed it to her every day. Her enthusiasm for the dessert inspired me to try a slice (up until that point in my life, I had avoided cream cheese altogether), and I'll never forget that first bite: the creamy, tangy center, the crunch from the graham cracker, the hit of chocolate ganache all made time stand still for three glorious seconds. I've been hooked ever since.

White Chocolate Cheesecake

MAKES · ONE 9 IN
[23 CM] CAKE

79

CRUST

2 cups [200 g] graham cracker crumbs

2 tablespoons granulated sugar

5 tablespoons [70 g] unsalted butter, melted

CHEESECAKE

2 lb [900 g] cream cheese, at room temperature

1 cup [200 g] granulated sugar

½ teaspoon salt

1 cup [240 g] Crème Fraîche (page 278) or store-bought

2 tablespoons unsalted butter, melted and cooled to room temperature

1 tablespoon pure vanilla extract

3 large eggs, at room temperature

1 large egg yolk, at room temperature

¾ cup [180 g] heavy cream, at room temperature

8 oz [226 g] white chocolate, melted and cooled

1 recipe Whipped Cream (page 278), caramel variation (optional)

1) **FOR THE CRUST** Position an oven rack in the middle of the oven and preheat the oven to 325°F [170°C]. Grease a 9 in [23 cm] spring-form pan. 2) In a medium bowl, mix together the graham cracker crumbs and granulated sugar. Add the melted butter and stir until all the crumbs are coated. Use a measuring cup or spoon to press the crumbs evenly onto the bottom of the prepared pan. 3) Bake for 12 to 15 minutes, until lightly browned and fragrant. Transfer the pan to a wire rack and let cool slightly. After the pan has cooled, wrap the outer sides in two layers of aluminum foil, with the shiny side facing out (this helps keep the sides of the cheesecake from browning). 4) **FOR THE CHEESECAKE** In the bowl of a stand mixer fitted with a paddle, beat the cream cheese on medium speed until light and completely smooth, 4 to 5 minutes. Scrape down the sides of the bowl often, making sure all the cream cheese is silky smooth. Add the granulated sugar and salt and beat on medium speed until completely incorporated, stopping to scrape down the sides of the bowl as needed, 2 to 3 minutes.

cont'd

Add the crème fraîche, butter, and vanilla and beat on medium speed for 2 to 3 minutes. Add the eggs one at a time, then the yolk, beating on low speed after each addition until just combined. Add the heavy cream and mix on low speed until combined. Add the melted chocolate and mix on low speed until combined. Using a spatula, give the filling a couple of turns to make sure the white chocolate is completely incorporated. Pour the filling over the cooled crust and use an offset spatula to smooth the top. Tap the bottom of the pan on the counter a few times to help get rid of any air bubbles. 5) Set a large roasting pan on the floor of the oven and fill it with 4 qt [3.8 L] of boiling water (see notes at right). Place the springform pan on the oven rack and bake the cheesecake for 1 hour without opening the door. Check the cheesecake after 1 hour; the outer ring (2 to 3 in [5 to 7.5 cm]) of the cheesecake should be slightly puffed and fairly firm, and the center should be set but still a bit jiggly when wiggled gently, resembling Jell-O. If the outer ring is not firm, let the cheesecake bake another 10 to 15 minutes (see notes at right). The center of the cheesecake should register 150°F [65°C]. Turn off the heat, open the oven door just a crack, and let the cheesecake rest and cool in the warm, humid oven for 30 minutes. 6) Transfer the pan to a wire rack and let cool for 5 to 10 minutes. Remove the foil from the pan and carefully run a thin knife or an offset spatula around the cake to help loosen it from the pan (this will prevent cracking as it cools). Once the cake is completely cool, place a piece of parchment paper over the top of the pan (to keep condensation off the top of the

cheesecake) and transfer to the refrigerator. Let chill for at least 6 hours or overnight. 7) TO ASSEMBLE To remove the cheesecake from the pan, run a thin, offset spatula between the sides of the cake and the pan and then gently remove the sides. Slide the spatula between the bottom of the crust and the pan to loosen it, then carefully slide the cheesecake onto a serving plate. Let the cheesecake come to room temperature before serving. Top with the whipped cream. The cheesecake can be stored in in the refrigerator, covered, for up to 2 days.

NOTES I've always used a roasting pan of water on the floor of the oven instead of immersing the cheesecake in a water bath. The steam from the water helps prevent the cheesecake from drying and cracking. Many people argue that a water bath helps create a creamier cheesecake, but I haven't noticed a significant difference, and I find this method less worrisome than trying to stick a springform in water and then moving it to the oven.

The baking time on the cheesecake is relative, and it may take longer to bake than suggested. Making sure your ingredients are room temperature, adding boiling water to the roasting pan, and using an oven thermometer to make sure your oven temperature is correct will ensure good results. Don't be afraid to bake your cheesecake longer than noted if it hasn't set; this will not hurt the cheesecake.

"But I don't mind some cake—seed-cake, if you have any." "Lots!" Bilbo found himself answering, to his surprise; and he found himself scuttling off, too, to the cellar to fill a pint-beer mug, and then to a pantry to fetch two beautiful round seed-cakes which he had baked that afternoon for his after-supper morsel."

These picnic cakes always remind me of this scene in J. R. R. Tolkien's *The Hobbit*; they are small, simple treats that can be wrapped up and slipped into a backpack or picnic basket and are perfect for nibbling on and sharing with other afternoon wanderers.

Picnic Cakes

MAKES · THREE 6 IN
[15 CM] CAKES

1⅓ cups [189 g] all-purpose flour

¼ cup [25 g] almond flour

2 tablespoons poppy seeds

¾ teaspoon baking powder

¾ teaspoon salt

½ teaspoon baking soda

8 tablespoons [1 stick or 113 g] unsalted butter, at room temperature

1 cup [200 g] granulated sugar, plus more for sprinkling

2 large eggs, at room temperature

1½ teaspoons almond extract, more or less to taste

1 teaspoon pure vanilla extract

½ cup [120 g] sour cream, at room temperature

½ cup [120 g] buttermilk, at room temperature

1 cup [100 g] sliced almonds (optional)

Confectioners' sugar, for dusting (optional)

1) Position an oven rack in the middle of the oven and preheat the oven to 350°F [180°C]. Grease and flour three 6 in [15 cm] baking pans and line the bottoms with parchment paper. 2) In a medium bowl, whisk together the all-purpose flour, almond flour, poppy seeds, baking powder, salt, and baking soda.

cont'd

80

3) In the bowl of a stand mixer fitted with a paddle, beat the butter on medium speed until creamy, about 1 minute. Add the granulated sugar and mix again until light and fluffy, 4 to 6 minutes. Scrape down the sides of the bowl and add the eggs, one at a time, mixing on low speed until incorporated. Add the almond extract and vanilla and mix again until combined. Add one-third of the flour mixture, then the sour cream, mixing after each addition until just incorporated. Add half of the remaining flour mixture, then the buttermilk, and then the remaining flour mixture, mixing after each addition until just incorporated into the batter. Use a spatula to scrape down the bowl and make sure the mixture is completely combined. 4) Divide the batter among the prepared pans and use the back of a spoon or an offset spatula to smooth the tops. Generously sprinkle the top of each cake with granulated sugar, then cover with almonds (if using). Tap the pans gently on the counter twice each to help get rid of any air bubbles. 5) Bake for 24 to 30 minutes, rotating the pans halfway through, until the cakes are golden brown and a wooden skewer or toothpick inserted in the centers comes out clean. Transfer the pans to a wire rack and let cool for 3 or 4 minutes. Run a knife gently around the edge of the cakes to help release them from the sides, then let the cakes continue cooling in the pans until just warm, about 15 minutes. Run a knife gently around the sides again, then turn the cakes out onto the rack, remove the parchment paper, and let cool completely. Dust with confectioners' sugar (if using) and serve. The cakes can be stored in an airtight container at room temperature for up to 3 days.

Technically this is an oversized Toaster Strudel (something my mom refused to let us eat on a regular basis growing up, no matter how much we begged), but since we are baking a pastry and not jamming it in the toaster I have changed up the title. My Rough Puff Pastry (page 268) makes for a flaky treat, and you can choose the filling that suits your mood. Sprinkles are optional, but way more fun.

Giant Pop Tart

MAKES · 12 LARGE OR 24 SMALL SQUARES

CREAM CHEESE FILLING

4 oz [113 g] cream cheese, at room temperature

3 tablespoons granulated sugar

¼ teaspoon salt

1 teaspoon pure vanilla extract

½ cup [112 g] jam, apple butter, Nutella, or peanut butter

ASSEMBLY

All-purpose flour, for dusting

1 recipe Rough Puff Pastry (page 268), cut into two equal pieces

Egg wash (see page 16)

ICING

2 to 4 tablespoons milk

2 tablespoons unsalted butter, melted

½ teaspoon pure vanilla extract

Pinch of salt

1½ cups [180 g] confectioners' sugar

Sprinkles, for decorating (optional)

1) **FOR THE CREAM CHEESE FILLING** In the bowl of a stand mixer fitted with a paddle, beat the cream cheese on medium speed until smooth and creamy, 2 to 3 minutes. Add the granulated sugar and salt and beat again until smooth. With the mixer running on low speed, add the vanilla and mix until completely combined, stopping to scrape down the sides of the bowl as needed. Refrigerate until ready to use.

2) **TO ASSEMBLE** Lightly flour a large sheet of parchment paper and roll half of the dough into a 9 by 13 in [23 by 33 cm] rectangle. Repeat with the second piece of dough. Keeping the parchment paper in place under the dough, transfer one rectangle to a baking sheet. Using an offset spatula, spread the cream cheese filling over the top of the pastry, leaving a 1 in [2.5 cm] border. Top the cream cheese with

the jam. Using the parchment paper, place the second rectangle of dough on top of the filling and discard the parchment. Pinch the edges of the dough together, then crimp the edges with a fork. Place the pan in the freezer for about 20 minutes while the oven is preheating. You want the dough to be nice and firm before you bake it. 3) Position an oven rack in the middle of the oven and preheat the oven to 400°F [200°C]. 4) When ready to bake, brush the top of the dough with egg wash. Bake 30 to 40 minutes, until the crust is deep golden brown and puffed. Transfer the strudel in its pan to a wire rack and let cool before icing. 5) FOR THE ICING In a medium bowl, whisk together 2 tablespoons of the milk, the melted butter, vanilla, and salt until smooth. Add the confectioners' sugar and mix together, then whisk until well combined and smooth. Add more milk, 1 tablespoon at a time, to thin the icing to your preferred consistency; the icing should be thick but pourable. Pour the icing over the top, using the back of a spoon or an offset spatula to smooth the icing. Scatter sprinkles over the top (if using). Let the icing set, then cut into squares and serve. The strudel is best eaten the same day it's made.

81

My good friend Zoë François created the most beautiful pavlova I have ever seen, a work of art filled with whipped cream and passion fruit. Drawing on the origin of the dessert with the dancer Anna Pavlova, Zoë innovated a tutu shape for her pavlovas that has become her signature. Like with my Smoky Butterscotch Cream Pie (page 112), I chose an easier route for my version of her recipe. I make small circles of pavlova, which bake up faster, and I pile them full of fruity goodness to cover any cracks.

Pavlova

MAKES • 5 OR 6 PAVLOVAS

1 recipe Meringue (page 258), doubled, pavlova variation

1 recipe Pastry Cream (page 279)

1 recipe Lemon Curd (page 282)

1 recipe Whipped Cream (page 278)

Fresh berries, for topping

Passion fruit pulp, for topping

Chopped fresh herbs, such as mint, anise hyssop, or rose geranium, for topping

Confectioners' sugar, for sprinkling (optional)

1) Position an oven rack in the middle of the oven and preheat the oven to 275°F [135°C]. Line a sheet pan with parchment paper. **2)** Place a 4 by 2 in [10 by 5 cm] ring mold on the parchment paper and fill it with meringue, smoothing the top with an offset spatula. Carefully remove the mold. (If you do not have a ring mold, you can shape a 4 by 2 in [10 by 5 cm] circle freeform on the parchment.) Repeat this on the parchment paper 8 times, spacing the circles out with a few inches between each one (they will spread as they bake). **3)** Bake until the pavlovas are light blond in color, 35 to 45 minutes. Turn off the oven and let the pavlovas sit in the oven for

2 hours. **4)** Remove from the oven, then use the back of a spoon or a paring knife to gently collapse the center of the pavlovas if they haven't already. Fill each with ¼ cup [56 g] of the pastry cream and ¼ cup [56 g] of the lemon curd. Top with the whipped cream, fresh berries, passion fruit pulp, fresh herbs, and a sprinkle of confectioners' sugar, if desired. Pavlovas are best eaten the same day they are made.

82

This giant croissant was inspired by the *New York Times* food section, after having seen Sohla El-Waylly's beautiful version. Here I use my Cheater Croissant Dough (page 264) and fill the croissant with apricot jam and frangipane, then top with almonds.

Apricot Almond Croissant

MAKES · 12 LARGE OR 24 SMALL SERVINGS

ASSEMBLY

All-purpose flour, for dusting

½ recipe Cheater Croissant Dough (page 264)

1 recipe Almond Cream (page 281)

1 cup [320 g] store-bought apricot jam

Egg wash (see page 16)

1 cup [100 g] sliced almonds

Confectioners' sugar, for dusting

1) Line a sheet pan with parchment paper. 2) Lightly flour a work surface and roll the dough into a 20 by 12 in [48 by 30 cm] rectangle. Spread the almond cream evenly over the top of the dough, followed by the jam. Fold the dough in half to make a 10 by 12 in [25 by 30 cm] rectangle. Use a rolling pin to gently compress the edges, then transfer the dough to the prepared pan. Cover the pan loosely with plastic wrap and let rise at room temperature until doubled in size, 1½ to 2 hours. 3) Position an oven rack in the middle of the oven and preheat the oven to 400°F [200°C].

4) Remove the plastic wrap, brush the dough with egg wash, then top with the almonds. 5) Bake for 25 to 35 minutes, rotating the pan halfway through, until the crust is deep golden brown and puffed. Carefully transfer the croissant to a wire rack and let cool until just warm to the touch (letting it cool off the pan will help it stay crisp on the bottom). Dust with confectioners' sugar, then slice and serve. The croissant is best eaten the same day it is made.

83

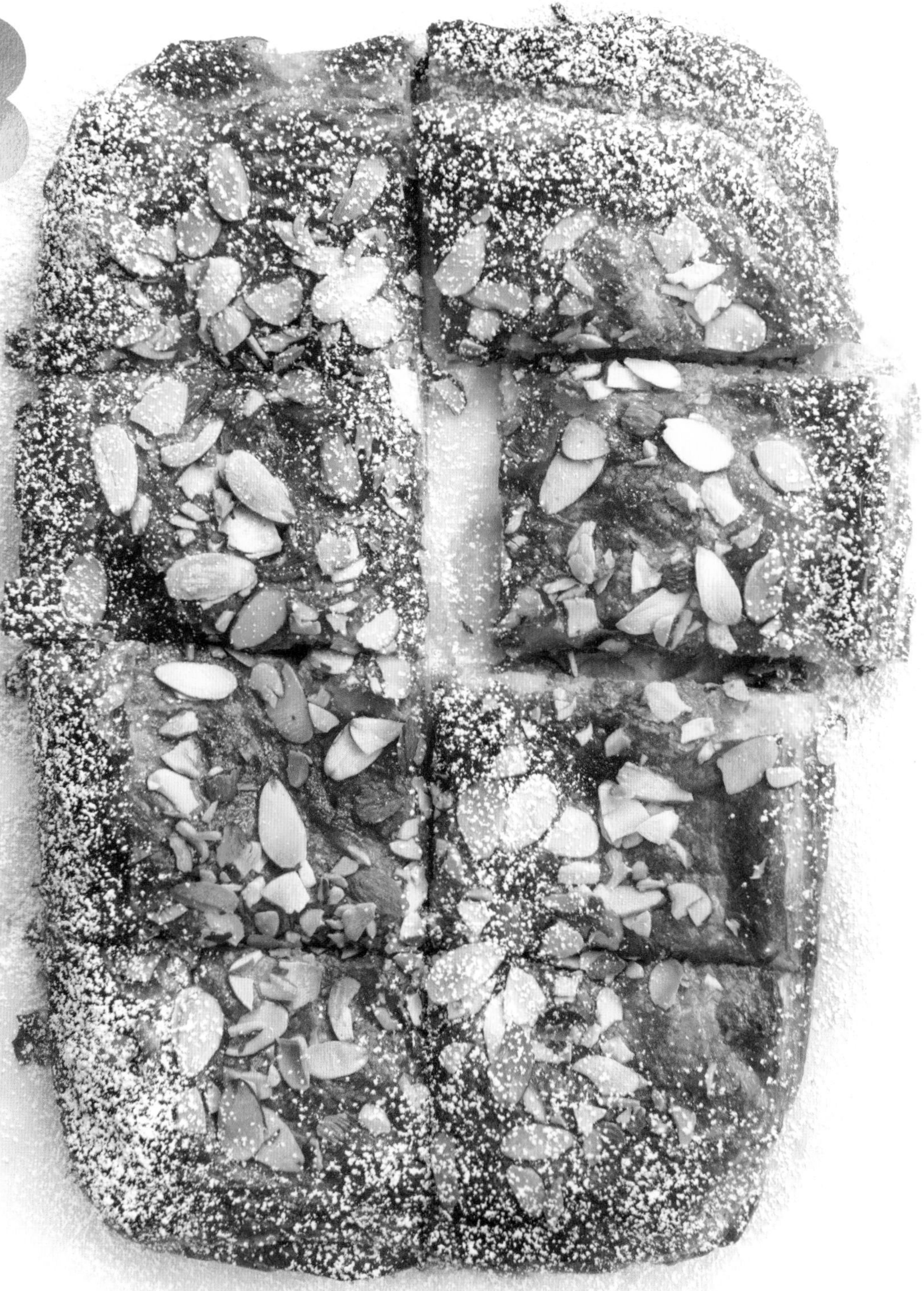

Over the years, more and more friends and family have found themselves gluten intolerant, and I wanted to come up with a simple cake that I could serve them for birthdays, holidays, or just because. Baking with gluten-free flours can be tricky, and I spent months working on this recipe. I didn't want to have to use a specific all-purpose gluten-free flour brand that may not be available everywhere, so I kept my base simple with just white rice flour and almond flour. After many tries, hours reading Reddit threads on gluten-free baking, and then coming across the book *Experimental Food Science* by Marjorie P. Penfield and Ada Marie Campbell, I finally had my cake.

My family (who is not gluten-free) *loves* this cake, and we love it plain, with no topping or frosting. It is a perfect afternoon snacking cake. However, whipped cream and strawberries are delicious on top, as is chocolate ganache poured over the cooled cake.

MAKES · ONE 8
IN [20 CM] CAKE

Gluten-Free Cake

1 cup [140 g]
white rice flour

1 cup [100 g]
almond flour

1¾ teaspoons baking
powder

¾ teaspoon salt

¼ teaspoon baking soda

3 large eggs, at room
temperature

1 large egg yolk,
at room temperature

1 tablespoon lemon juice

1 cup [200 g]
granulated sugar

1 tablespoon
pure vanilla extract

⅓ cup [75 g] vegetable
or canola oil

½ cup [120 g] buttermilk,
at room temperature

1) Position an oven rack in the middle of the oven and preheat the oven to 350°F [180°C]. Grease and line an 8 in [20 cm] baking pan. 2) In a medium bowl, whisk together the rice flour, almond flour, baking powder, salt, and baking soda. 3) In the bowl of a stand mixer fitted with a whisk, whisk the eggs, egg yolk, and lemon juice together on medium speed until foamy, about 1 minute. With the mixer still running, slowly sprinkle the granulated sugar into the egg mixture. Increase the speed to high and whip until the mixture has doubled

in volume and is thick and pale yellow, 4 to 5 minutes. 4) Lower the speed to low and add the vanilla, then slowly pour in the oil, followed by the buttermilk. Mix until incorporated, about 30 seconds. Add the flour mixture to the batter and mix on low speed for 90 seconds. Remove the bowl from the mixer and use the whisk attachment to gently whisk the batter, making sure all the ingredients are incorporated. Pour the mixture into the prepared pan.

5) Bake the cake until golden brown and a wooden skewer or toothpick inserted into the cake comes out clean, 35 to 40 minutes. Transfer the pan to a wire rack and let cool for 20 minutes. Run a knife around the edges of the pan, then turn the cake out onto the rack, remove the parchment paper, and let cool completely. This cake can be stored in an airtight container, at room temperature, for up to 3 days.

84

CHAPTER 7

Beginnings and Ends

"I have **heard what the talkers** were **talking,** the talk of the **beginning** and the **end,** But **I do not talk** of the **beginning** or the **end."**

—Walt Whitman, *Leaves of Grass*

This is a basic vanilla Swiss meringue buttercream—
with variations—that can be doubled for layer cakes.

Swiss Meringue Buttercream

MAKES · ABOUT
3 CUPS [720 G]

**A few drops
lemon juice**

**1¼ cups [250 g]
granulated sugar**

**⅔ cup [150 g] egg whites
(from 4 or 5 large eggs),
at room temperature**

¼ teaspoon salt

**¼ teaspoon cream of
tartar**

**2 cups [4 sticks or 455 g]
unsalted butter, at room
temperature**

**1 tablespoon
pure vanilla extract**

1) In a medium saucepan over medium heat, bring 1 in [2.5 cm] of water to a gentle boil. **2)** Pour the lemon juice into the bowl of a stand mixer and use a paper towel to wipe the juice around the inside of the bowl (this helps remove any trace of grease, which can hinder the whites from whipping properly). Add the granulated sugar, egg whites, salt, and cream of tartar and stir gently with a rubber spatula until completely combined. **3)** Place the bowl over the saucepan, being careful not to let the water touch the bottom of the bowl. Stir with the spatula for 4 to 5 minutes, until the sugar is completely dissolved and the mixture registers 160°F [70°C] on an instant-read thermometer, scraping down the sides of the bowl with the spatula (to ensure no

sugar crystals are lurking, which can cook the egg whites). **4)** Place the bowl in the stand mixer fitted with a whisk and whisk the egg whites on low speed for 1 minute. Slowly increase the speed to medium-high and beat for 8 to 10 minutes, until stiff peaks form. The bowl should feel cool to the touch at this point. **5)** Lower the speed to low and, with the mixer running, add 1 to 2 tablespoons of butter at a time, beating well after each addition. When the butter has been completely incorporated, add the vanilla and beat on low speed until incorporated. Use immediately or cover and refrigerate for up to 2 days. When ready to use, let the buttercream come to room temperature, then beat again in the stand mixer until smooth.

85

NOTES The butter needs to be added slowly to help it emulsify correctly into the meringue. Butter should be soft but cool when added, 68°F to 70°F [20°C to 21°C]. At any point, the buttercream may look curdled and runny, but this is normal. Keep adding the rest of the butter, and the buttercream will eventually turn smooth. If the buttercream is runny after beating, it may be that your butter or egg whites are too warm. Place the mixer bowl in the refrigerator for about 10 minutes, stirring the buttercream every couple minutes. Then whisk again until smooth.

VARIATIONS

• **Raspberry, Strawberry, or Blueberry Buttercream:** *Add ½ cup [32 g] of sifted freeze-dried raspberry, strawberry, or blueberry powder to the egg white mixture. Add 2 tablespoons of raspberry, strawberry, or blueberry vodka along with the vanilla.*

• **Brown Sugar Buttercream:** *Replace the granulated sugar in the recipe with brown sugar.*

While I love a proper Swiss meringue buttercream, sometimes there isn't enough time to make it. This faster version is a good substitute—buttery and creamy, without all the effort—and this recipe can be doubled or tripled.

American Buttercream

MAKES • ABOUT
2 CUPS [480 G]

1 cup [2 sticks or 227 g] unsalted butter, at room temperature

¼ teaspoon salt

1 tablespoon corn syrup

1½ cups [180 g] confectioners' sugar

1 tablespoon pure vanilla extract

In the bowl of a stand mixer fitted with a paddle, beat the butter and salt on medium speed until smooth and creamy. Scrape down the sides of the bowl and add the corn syrup, mixing on low speed until combined. Slowly add the confectioners' sugar, a little at a time, mixing until combined and stopping to scrape down the sides of the bowl as necessary. Add the vanilla and mix until smooth, then increase the speed to medium-low and mix for 6 to 8 minutes, until smooth, light, and creamy. Use immediately or cover and refrigerate for up to 2 days. When ready to use, let the buttercream come to room temperature, then beat again in the stand mixer until smooth.

VARIATIONS

• **Espresso Buttercream:** *Add 1 teaspoon of espresso grounds along with the salt. Add 2 tablespoons of brewed espresso and 1 tablespoon of Kahlúa (optional) along with the vanilla.*

• **Raspberry Buttercream:** *Add ⅓ cup [24 g] of sifted freeze-dried raspberry powder along with the salt. Add 2 tablespoons of raspberry vodka along with the vanilla.*

86

This buttercream method is an old-school, boiled-flour, less-sweet-than-traditional frosting that I fell in love with years ago. The method lends itself particularly well to infusing flavors (see variations that follow).

Ermine Buttercream

MAKES · ABOUT
2 CUPS [480 G]

¾ cup [150 g] granulated sugar

¼ cup [36 g] all-purpose flour

¼ teaspoon salt

½ cup [120 g] whole milk

½ cup [120 g] half-and-half

1 cup [2 sticks or 227 g] unsalted butter, at room temperature

2 teaspoons pure vanilla extract

Food coloring (optional)

1) In a medium bowl, whisk together the granulated sugar, flour, and salt until fully combined (the sugar will help keep the flour from lumping when it boils, so spend a good minute really whisking it together). Transfer the mixture into a medium, heavy-bottom saucepan. Slowly pour the whole milk and half-and-half into the pan, whisking constantly to combine as you pour. Cook over medium heat, stirring constantly, just until the mixture comes to a gentle boil (periodically run a spatula round the edges of the saucepan to remove any flour lurking there).

cont'd

87

Lower the heat to medium-low and continue to whisk constantly and stir the edges occasionally for 2 to 3 minutes, until the mixture has thickened considerably. It should be glossy and leave streaks in the bottom of the pan when you drag a spatula through it. Remove from the heat and continue stirring for 30 seconds. 2) Transfer the mixture to a bowl and cover with plastic wrap, making sure the plastic sits directly on top of the cream (this will help keep it from forming a skin). Let cool to room temperature. 3) When the flour mixture has cooled, place the butter in the bowl of a stand mixer fitted with a paddle. Beat on medium speed until smooth and creamy, stopping to scrape down the sides of the bowl as needed. Start adding the cooled flour mixture a few spoonfuls at a time, mixing on low speed after each addition, until it is all incorporated. Scrape down the sides and mix on medium speed for 2 to 3 minutes, until the buttercream is light and fluffy. Add the vanilla and food coloring (if using) and mix on low speed until combined. Use immediately or cover and refrigerate for up to 2 days. When ready to use, let the buttercream come to room temperature, then beat again in the stand mixer until smooth.

VARIATIONS

• **Basil Buttercream:** *Combine the milk, half-and-half, and 1 cup [12 g] of basil leaves in a medium saucepan. Heat gently over medium heat until just simmering, then remove from the heat. Let cool, then cover and refrigerate for at least 2 hours and up to overnight. Strain the basil from the milk, squeezing all the liquid out of the leaves, then discard. Add the infused milk to the buttercream as directed in step 1.*

• **Cardamom Buttercream:** *Combine the milk, half-and-half, and seeds from 10 black or green cardamom pods in a medium saucepan. Heat gently over medium heat until just simmering, then remove from the heat. Let cool, then cover and refrigerate for at least 2 hours and up to overnight. Strain the cardamom seeds from the milk and discard. Add the infused milk to the buttercream as directed in step 1.*

• **Coconut Buttercream:** *Replace the ½ cup [120 g] of whole milk and ½ cup [120 g] of half-and-half with 1 cup [240 g] of coconut milk. Add 2 teaspoons of coconut extract along with the vanilla.*

• **Green Tea or Coffee Buttercream:** *Combine the milk, half-and-half, and ½ cup [16 g] of green tea leaves (or two tea bags) or ½ cup [45 g] of whole coffee beans in a medium saucepan. Heat gently over medium heat until just simmering, then remove from the heat. Let cool, then cover and refrigerate for at least 2 hours and up to overnight. Strain the solids from the milk and discard. Add the infused milk to the buttercream as directed in step 1. For the coffee variation, add 1 teaspoon of finely ground espresso with the vanilla in step 3 (optional).*

• **Malt Buttercream:** *Add ½ cup [54 g] of malt powder to the saucepan along with the granulated sugar.*

• **Rosemary or Lavender Buttercream:** *Combine the milk, half-and-half, and 2 rosemary sprigs or 1 teaspoon of culinary lavender in a medium saucepan. Heat gently over medium heat until just simmering, then remove from the heat. Let cool, then cover and refrigerate for at least 2 hours and up to overnight. Strain the solids from the milk and discard. Add the infused milk to the buttercream as directed in step 1.*

Inspired by Zoë François, who was inspired by Flo Braker, this buttercream
is exactly as its name describes: ultra. Ultra-rich, ultra-buttery,
and ultra-smooth, it is a dream to eat with any cake.

Ultra Buttercream

MAKES · ABOUT
3 CUPS [720 G]

5 large egg yolks, at
room temperature

1 cup [200 g] granulated
sugar

¼ cup [60 g] water

¼ teaspoon salt

1 cup [2 sticks or 227 g]
unsalted butter, at room
temperature

1½ teaspoons pure
vanilla extract

1) In the bowl of a stand mixer fitted with a paddle, beat the egg yolks on low speed. With the mixer running on low speed, slowly add ¼ cup [50 g] of the granulated sugar and increase the speed to medium. Beat the egg-sugar mixture for about 5 minutes, until very thick and pale yellow. 2) In a medium, heavy-bottom saucepan, combine the remaining ¾ cup [150 g] of sugar, the water, and salt. Stir over medium heat until the sugar is dissolved. Increase the heat to high and bring the mixture to a boil over medium-high heat until the temperature reaches 240°F [115°C], 4 to 5 minutes. 3) With the stand mixer running on low speed, carefully pour the hot syrup along the inside of the mixing bowl, being careful not to hit the whisk. When all the syrup is in the bowl, increase the speed to medium-high and continue

whisking for 8 to 10 minutes, until the mixture has doubled in volume and is quite thick and glossy, and the sides of the bowl have cooled. Lower the speed to low and, with the mixer running, add 1 to 2 tablespoons of butter at a time, beating well after each addition. When the butter has been completely incorporated, add the vanilla. Beat on low speed until incorporated, then use immediately or cover and refrigerate for up to 2 days. When ready to use, let the buttercream come to room temperature, then beat again in the stand mixer until smooth.

VARIATION
• **Irish Cream Ultra Buttercream:** *After adding the vanilla, slowly add ¼ cup [60 g] of Irish cream to the buttercream as it is beating, and mix to combine.*

This icing, with its subtle tang and balanced sweetness, is used in a variety of combinations throughout this book: with pumpkin spice, banana, sugar cookie, and of course red velvet. To make twice as much for a larger cake or pan of bars, simply double the recipe.

Cream Cheese Buttercream

MAKES • 2 OR 3 CUPS [480 OR 720 G], FOR AN 8 OR 9 IN [20 OR 23 CM] CAKE

89

4 oz [113 g] cream cheese, at room temperature

4 tablespoons [56 g] unsalted butter, at room temperature

⅛ teaspoon salt

2 cups [240 g] confectioners' sugar

1 teaspoon pure vanilla extract

In the bowl of a stand mixer fitted with a paddle, beat the cream cheese, butter, and salt on low speed for 2 to 3 minutes, until smooth, creamy, and combined. Gradually add the confectioners' sugar and mix on low speed until combined and smooth, stopping to scrape down the sides of the bowl as necessary. Use immediately or cover and refrigerate for up to 2 days. When ready to use, let the buttercream come to room temperature, then beat again in the stand mixer until smooth.

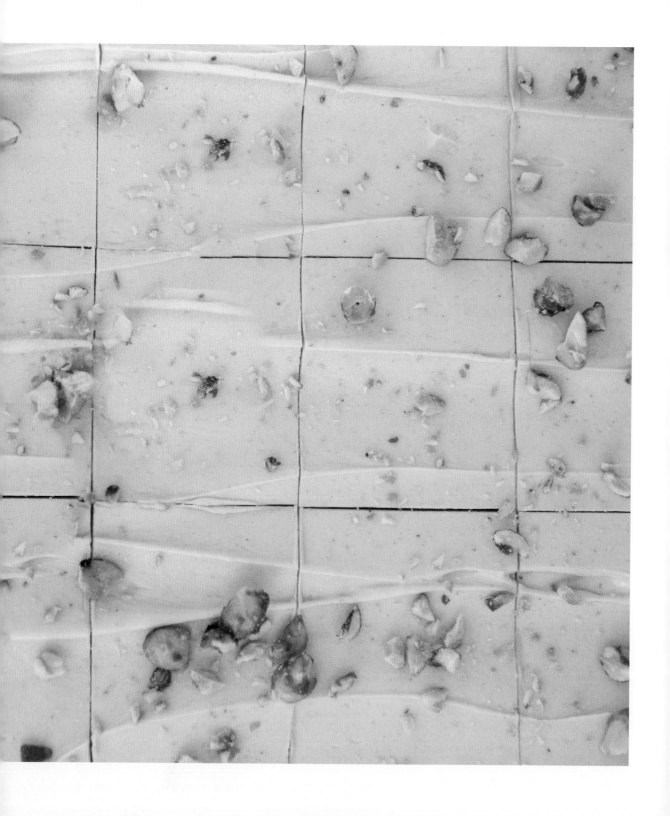

I adore this buttercream, and especially love it on top
of the chocolate sheet cake (page 196). The tiny bit of lemon juice
brightens the flavor of the peanut butter.

Peanut Butter Buttercream

MAKES · 3 CUPS
[720 G]

1 cup [2 sticks or 227 g] unsalted butter, at room temperature

½ cup [108 g] creamy peanut butter

¼ teaspoon salt

2 cups [240 g] confectioners' sugar

1 teaspoon pure vanilla extract

¼ teaspoon lemon juice

In the bowl of a stand mixer fitted with a paddle, beat the butter, peanut butter, and salt on medium speed for about 3 minutes, until light yellow and fluffy. Lower the speed to low and gradually add the confectioners' sugar. Beat on medium speed, stopping to scrape down the sides of the bowl as necessary, for 2 to 3 minutes, until smooth and creamy. Add the vanilla and lemon juice and mix on low speed until combined. Use a rubber spatula to mix the frosting a few more times, making sure it is completely combined. Use immediately or cover and refrigerate for up to 2 days. When ready to use, let the buttercream come to room temperature, then beat again in the stand mixer until smooth.

90

This buttercream is rich and creamy, with plenty of chocolate flavor.

MAKES · 3 CUPS
[720 G]

Bittersweet Chocolate Buttercream

6 oz [170 g] bittersweet chocolate

1 cup [2 sticks or 227 g] unsalted butter, at room temperature

Pinch of salt

2 tablespoons corn syrup

1 teaspoon pure vanilla extract

1½ cups [180 g] confectioners' sugar

1) In a medium saucepan over medium heat, bring 1 in [2.5 cm] of water to a gentle boil. Place the chocolate in a heatproof bowl and set it over the pan of boiling water, being careful not to let the water touch the bottom of the bowl. Stir constantly until just melted, then set aside to cool slightly. 2) In the bowl of a stand mixer fitted with a paddle, beat the butter and salt on medium speed for about 3 minutes, until light yellow and fluffy. Add the corn syrup and vanilla and beat on medium speed until combined. Lower the speed to low and gradually add the confectioners' sugar. Beat on medium speed, stopping to scrape down the sides of the bowl as necessary, for 2 to 3 minutes, until smooth and creamy. Add the chocolate and mix on low speed until no streaks remain. Use a rubber spatula to mix the frosting a few more times, making sure it is completely combined. Use immediately or cover and refrigerate for up to 2 days. When ready to use, let the buttercream come to room temperature and then beat again in the stand mixer until smooth.

91

Perfectly fudgy and delicious on any cake, this thick, decadent spread
works especially well on Classic Birthday Cake (page 52).

Fudge Buttercream

MAKES • ABOUT 4 CUPS [775 G]
BUTTERCREAM

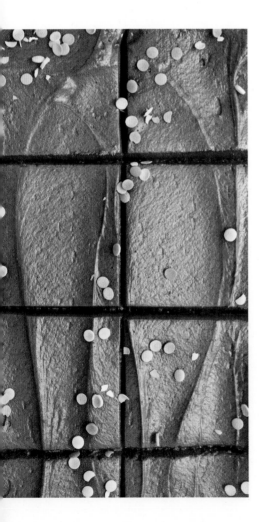

1 cup [2 sticks or 227 g]
unsalted butter, at room
temperature

⅔ cup [65 g] Dutch-
process cocoa powder

2 tablespoons corn syrup

1 teaspoon
pure vanilla extract

Pinch of salt

¼ cup [60 g] milk, at
room temperature

¼ cup [60 g] Crème
Fraîche (page 278), at
room temperature

3 cups [360 g]
confectioners' sugar

92

In the bowl of a stand mixer fitted
with a paddle, beat the butter on
medium speed for 2 to 3 minutes,
until creamy. Add the cocoa powder, corn syrup, vanilla, and salt
and mix again on medium speed
for 2 to 3 minutes, until light and
creamy. Scrape down the sides of
the bowl, add the milk and crème
fraîche, and mix on low speed until
combined. Add the confectioners'
sugar and mix on medium speed
for 2 to 3 minutes, until combined.
The more you mix, the lighter the
frosting will get. Finish mixing with
a spatula, making sure all the
ingredients are evenly incorporated. Use immediately or cover
and refrigerate for up to 2 days.
When ready to use, let the buttercream come to room temperature,
then beat again in the stand mixer
until smooth.

Rich, delicious, and easy to make, ganache should be poured over everything.

Ganache

12 oz [340 g] semisweet or bittersweet chocolate, finely chopped

1½ cups [360 g] heavy cream

1) Place the chocolate in a medium heatproof bowl. Heat the heavy cream in a small saucepan until it is simmering and just about to boil. Pour the cream over the chocolate, cover the bowl with plastic wrap, and let sit for 5 minutes.

2) Remove the plastic and whisk until completely smooth. Use as directed in the recipe. Ganache can be stored in an airtight container in the refrigerator for up to 3 days. Bring to room temperature and gently reheat on the stovetop to use.

VARIATION
• *Half-Sheet Pan Ganache: Use 1 lb [455 g] bittersweet chocolate, finely chopped, and 2 cups [480 g] heavy cream.*

93

I grew up not liking meringue. My grandma topped her pretty pies with it constantly, but I found it sweet and bland and I avoided it at all costs. When I started making it myself, I became obsessed with the transformation of sugar and egg whites. Maybe it's the Minnesotan in me, but I find the snowy piles in my mixing bowl beautiful. A bit of salt and a hefty splash of vanilla helps keep this from tasting flat and overly sugary. This recipe can be doubled.

Meringue

MAKES · 2 CUPS
[240 G]

A few drops of lemon juice

1 cup [200 g] granulated sugar

½ cup [113 g] egg whites (from 3 or 4 large eggs), at room temperature

Pinch of salt

⅛ teaspoon cream of tartar

2 teaspoons pure vanilla extract

1) In a medium saucepan over medium heat, bring 1 in [2.5 cm] of water to a gentle boil. 2) Pour the lemon juice into the bowl of a stand mixer and use a paper towel to wipe the juice around the inside of the bowl (this helps remove any trace of grease, which can hinder the whites from whipping properly). Add the granulated sugar, egg whites, salt, and cream of tartar to the mixing bowl and stir gently with a rubber spatula until completely combined. 3) Place the bowl over the saucepan, being careful not to let the water touch the bottom of the bowl. Stir with the spatula until the sugar is completely dissolved and the mixture registers 160°F [70°C] on an instant-read thermometer,

scraping down the sides of the bowl with the spatula (to ensure no sugar crystals are lurking, which can cook the egg whites), 4 to 5 minutes. 4) Place the bowl in the stand mixer fitted with a whisk and whisk the egg whites on low speed for 1 minute, until foamy. Slowly increase the speed to medium-high and beat for 8 to 10 minutes until stiff, glossy peaks form. The bowl should feel cool to the touch at this point. Add the vanilla and mix on low speed until combined. 5) Use the meringue immediately. You can use the meringue unbaked to decorate at this point, or continue on with the recipe to make baked meringues.

VARIATIONS

• **Baked Meringues:** *Preheat the oven to 200°F [95°C]. Line two baking sheets with parchment paper. Working quickly, place the mixture into a pastry bag fitted with a ½ in [13 mm] tip. Pipe 1½ in [4 cm] mounds about 1 in [2.5 cm] apart on the prepared sheet pans, for 5 rows of 5 meringues on each sheet. Bake for 1 hour. Turn off the oven and let the meringues sit in the cooling oven for 1 hour more. Transfer the sheets to a wire rack and let the meringues cool completely. Store meringues in an airtight container at room temperature for up to 1 week.*

• **Brown Sugar Meringue:** *Replace the 1 cup [200 g] of granulated sugar with 1 cup [200 g] of brown sugar.*

• **Cacao Nib Meringue:** *Add ½ cup [60 g] of chopped cacao nibs to the meringues after adding the vanilla and use a spatula to combine.*

• **Pavlova:** *To make the Pavlova (page 233), use a double recipe of the meringue. Add 2 tablespoons of cornstarch and 2 teaspoons of white vinegar to the meringue along with the vanilla.*

I've been making this pie dough for many years; I love how flaky and rich it is. If your kitchen is especially warm, chill the dry ingredients for 10 minutes before moving to step 2.

MAKES • 2 SLAB
PIE CRUSTS

Pie Dough

18 tablespoons [2¼ sticks or 255 g] unsalted butter, cut into 18 pieces

3 cups [420 g] all-purpose flour, plus more for dusting

2 tablespoons granulated sugar

1 teaspoon salt

1 cup [240 g] ice water

1) Place the butter pieces in a small bowl and freeze for 5 to 10 minutes. 2) In the bowl of a stand mixer fitted with a paddle, mix the flour, granulated sugar, and salt on low speed until combined. Add half of the chilled butter and mix on low speed until the butter is just starting to break down, about 1 minute. Add the rest of the butter and continue mixing until the butter is broken down in various sizes (some butter will be incorporated into the dough, some pieces will be a bit large, but most should be about the size of small peas). Stop the mixer and use your hands to check for any dry patches of flour on the bottom of the bowl; incorporate the flour as best you can. 3) With the mixer running on low speed, slowly add about ¼ cup [60 g] of the ice water and

mix until the dough starts to come together but is still quite shaggy (if the dough is not coming together, add more water, 1 tablespoon at a time, until it does). 4) Transfer the dough to a lightly floured work surface and flatten it slightly into a square. Gather any loose/dry pieces that won't stick to the dough and place them on top of the square. Gently fold the dough over onto itself and then flatten into a square again. Repeat this process three or four more times until all the loose pieces are worked into the dough, being careful not to overwork the dough. Flatten the dough one last time, form it into two 6 in [15 cm] discs, and wrap the dough in plastic wrap. Refrigerate the dough for 30 minutes (and up to 2 days) before using.

This is a simple, pat-in-the-pan crust that comes in handy for many applications.

Pat-in-the-Pan Pie Dough

MAKES · ONE 8 OR 9 IN
[20 OR 23 CM] CRUST

1 cup [142 g] all-purpose flour

¼ cup [50 g] granulated sugar

¼ cup [30 g] almond flour

½ teaspoon salt

6 tablespoons [84 g] unsalted butter, at room temperature

2 tablespoons Crème Fraîche (page 278) or sour cream

96

1) In the bowl of a food processor fitted with a blade, pulse together the all-purpose flour, granulated sugar, almond flour, and salt until combined. Add the butter and crème fraîche and pulse until the dough starts to come together. (This dough is very forgiving, and you don't have to worry quite as much about overworking it as you do a normal pie dough.)

2) To bake, press the dough in the called-for pan. For a square pan, press the dough into an even thickness across the bottom. Bake the crust for 20 to 25 minutes at 350°F [180°C], until the dough is no longer wet to the touch. Transfer the pan to a wire rack and let cool completely.

3) For a pie pan, press the dough across the bottom and up the sides of the pan. Line the pan with parchment paper, covering the edges. Fill with pie weights, and bake for 20 to 25 minutes, until the dough is no longer wet to the touch. Remove the weights and the parchment paper, and return the pan to the oven for 3 to 4 minutes, until the crust is golden brown. Transfer the pan to a wire rack and let cool completely. (Pie weights are used for this pan to help the sides from slipping down as they bake).

VARIATION
• **Pecan Dough:** *Replace the almond flour with toasted, ground pecans.*

This crust is easy to handle and rich in flavor, with just enough tang to provide the perfect foil to Apple Cider Pie (page 118).

Crème Fraîche Dough

MAKES · ONE 8 OR 9 IN [20 OR 23 CM] CRUST

2 cups [284 g] all-purpose flour, plus more for dusting

¼ cup [50 g] granulated sugar

¾ teaspoon salt

1 cup [2 sticks or 227 g] unsalted butter, cold, cut into 16 pieces

¼ cup [60 g] Crème Fraîche (page 278) or sour cream

1) In a food processor fitted with a blade, combine the flour, granulated sugar, and salt. Add the butter and process for about 1 minute, until the butter breaks down and is incorporated into the dough. Add the crème fraîche and pulse until it is completely combined into the dough. Dump the dough onto a lightly floured work surface and gently fold the dough over onto itself until it comes together.

2) Form the pieces into two 6 in [15 cm] disks, wrap in plastic wrap, and refrigerate for at least 2 hours before using.

97

This dough is inspired by many recipes, but specifically Dominique Ansel's croissant MasterClass and Mandy Lee's laminated dough in her book *The Art of Escapism Cooking*. Mandy skips using the butter in a block, instead spreading room temperature butter over the surface of the dough, and then proceeds with the folding. The results are amazingly flaky and delicious.

Cheater Croissant Dough

MAKES · ABOUT 2½ LB [1.1 KG]

98

1½ cups [360 g] warm water (100°F to 110°F [35°C to 42°C])

1 tablespoon plus 1 teaspoon active dry yeast

4 cups plus 1 tablespoon [577 g] all-purpose flour, plus more for dusting

⅓ cup [65 g] granulated sugar

2 teaspoons salt

2 tablespoons unsalted butter, melted

1½ cups [3 sticks or 339 g] European butter (preferably 83 to 84 percent butterfat), at room temperature (68°F [20°C])

1) Grease a large bowl and set aside. In a small bowl or liquid measuring cup, stir together the water and yeast and let sit until the yeast has dissolved, about 5 minutes. 2) In the bowl of a stand mixer fitted with a dough hook, whisk together 4 cups [568 g] of the flour, the granulated sugar, and salt. Start the mixer on low speed and add the water-yeast mixture, followed by the melted butter. Continue to mix for 3 or 4 minutes, until all the ingredients are combined (see notes, page 265). The dough will be rough and bumpy, but it should be in one piece. Transfer the dough to the greased bowl and cover with plastic wrap. Let rise at room temperature until doubled in size, 1½ to 2 hours. 3) With your fist, gently press down on the dough, releasing as much gas as possible. Place the dough on a large piece of plastic wrap and shape into

a 10 by 12 in [25 by 30.5 cm] rectangle. Cover the dough with more plastic wrap, place it on a sheet pan, and refrigerate for at least 2 hours or overnight. 4) In the bowl of the stand mixer now fitted with a paddle, beat together the European butter and the remaining 1 tablespoon of flour for 2 to 3 minutes, until combined and creamy. The mixture should be pliable, but not melting; it should have the texture of cream cheese and should spread evenly. 5) Remove the dough from the refrigerator, unwrap it, and place it on a lightly floured work surface. Roll out the dough into a 12 by 20 in [30.5 by 50 cm] rectangle. Spread the entire rectangle evenly with the butter, leaving a ½ in [13 mm] border around the rectangle. Make the first turn, or letter fold: Starting with a short side facing you, fold one-third of the dough onto itself, making sure the edges are lined up with each other. Then fold the remaining one-third of the dough on top of the side that has already been folded. Rotate the dough so the seam is facing to the right and one open end is facing you. Gently roll out the dough into a 10 by 18 in [25 by 46 cm] rectangle. (Each time you roll, the rectangle will get a bit smaller.) Repeat the letter fold. Sprinkle flour on a sheet pan or plate, place the dough on it, and freeze the dough for 6 minutes—set a timer so you don't forget (see notes below)! 6) Remove the dough from the freezer and repeat the letter fold again, making sure the seam is facing to the right. Roll out the dough again into a rectangle, this time about 8 by 16 in [20 by 40.5 cm]. Repeat the steps for one letter fold. Gently compress the dough with the rolling pin, and depending on the recipe you are using it in, keep the dough in one piece or cut it into two equal portions. If using the dough immediately, place the piece being used in the freezer for 6 minutes to chill, then proceed with the recipe. Otherwise, wrap the dough in plastic wrap, place it in a freezer-safe bag, and freeze for up to 2 weeks. The dough can be removed from the freezer the night before using and placed in the refrigerator to thaw.

NOTES Don't overmix the dough when combining the ingredients; this can result in a tough, chewy texture.

If the dough is left in the freezer for more than 6 minutes, it will start to freeze and then break apart as you roll it out. If you didn't remove the dough on time, let it sit at room temperature for a while until it rolls out easily.

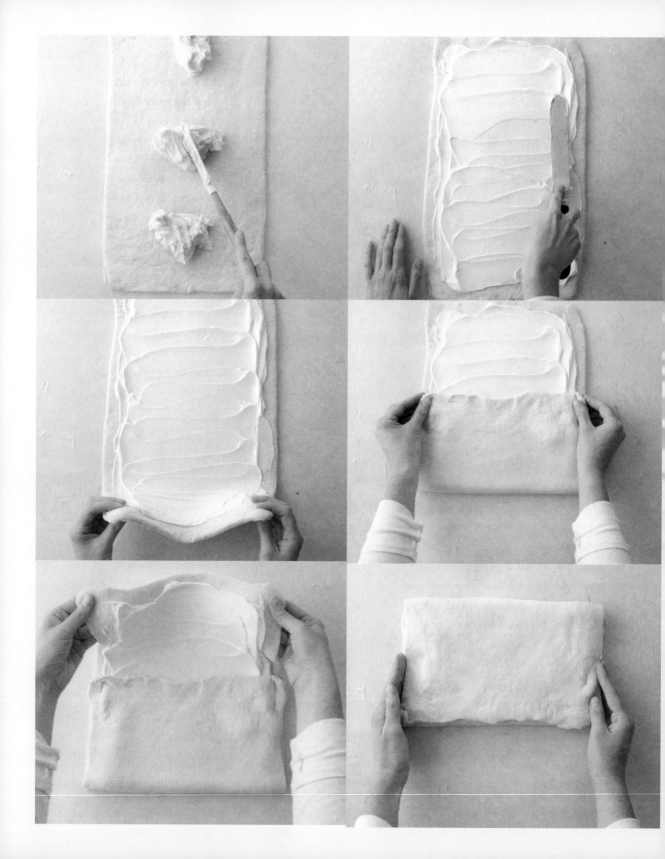

This is my shortcut to puff pastry, a recipe method less exacting and labor-intensive than the real thing. But you don't lose out on rich, flaky layers; this rough puff boasts those in spades.

Rough Puff Pastry

MAKES · ABOUT 2 LB [900 G]

2 cups [284 g] all-purpose flour, plus more for dusting

1½ cups [3 sticks or 339 g] unsalted butter, cut into 20 pieces

¼ cup [60 g] ice water, plus 1 to 2 tablespoons, as needed

½ teaspoon lemon juice

1 tablespoon granulated sugar

½ teaspoon salt

1) Dust a sheet pan or plate with flour and set aside. Place the butter pieces in a small bowl in the freezer for 5 to 10 minutes. 2) In a liquid measuring cup, combine ¼ cup [60 g] of the ice water and the lemon juice. 3) In the bowl of a stand mixer fitted with a paddle, mix together the flour, granulated sugar, and salt on low speed. Add the chilled butter and mix until only slightly incorporated. The pieces of butter will be smashed and in all different sizes, most about half their original size. Add the water mixture and mix until the dough just holds together and looks shaggy. If the dough is still really dry and not coming together, add more ice water, 1 tablespoon at a time, until the dough just starts to hold. 4) Transfer the dough to a lightly floured work surface and flatten it slightly into a square. Gather any dry, loose pieces and

place them on top of the square. Gently fold the dough over on itself and then flatten into a square again. Repeat this process five or six times, until all the loose pieces are worked into the dough. Flatten the dough one last time and form it into a 6 in [15 cm] square. Transfer the dough to the prepared sheet pan and sprinkle the dough with flour. Refrigerate for 20 minutes, until firm. 5) Return the dough to the lightly floured work surface and roll it into an 8 by 16 in [20 by 40.5 cm] rectangle. If the dough sticks at all, sprinkle more flour underneath it. Brush any excess flour off the dough and, using a bench scraper, fold the short ends of the dough over the middle, like a business letter, making three layers. This is the first turn. (If the dough still looks shaggy, don't worry; it will become smooth and will even out as you keep rolling.) 6) Flip the dough over, seam side down, give the dough a quarter turn, and

roll away from you, this time into a 6 by 16 in [15 by 40.5 cm] rectangle. Fold the short ends over the middle again, business-letter style. This is the second turn. Sprinkle the top of the dough with flour, return it to the sheet pan, and refrigerate for 20 minutes. 7) Return the dough to the work surface and repeat the process of folding the dough for the third and fourth turns. On the fourth turn, use a rolling pin to gently compress the layers together slightly. Depending on the recipe you are using it in, keep the dough in one piece or cut the dough into two equal portions. Wrap tightly in plastic wrap and refrigerate for at least 1 hour before using. Otherwise, wrap the dough in plastic wrap, place it in a freezer-safe bag, and freeze for up to 2 weeks. The dough can be removed from the freezer the night before using and placed in the refrigerator to thaw.

This recipe is a great homemade replacement for chocolate wafer cookies, which are often used in cookie crusts. It makes a large batch and also freezes well, so you can always have cookies on hand if needed.

MAKES · ABOUT
50 COOKIES

Chocolate Wafer Cookies

1 cup plus 2 tablespoons [160 g] all-purpose flour

½ cup [50 g] Dutch-process cocoa powder, plus more for dusting

½ teaspoon salt

½ teaspoon baking soda

8 tablespoons [1 stick or 113 g] unsalted butter, at room temperature

½ cup [100 g] granulated sugar

¼ cup [50 g] brown sugar

1 teaspoon pure vanilla extract

3 tablespoons heavy cream

1) In a small bowl, combine the flour, cocoa powder, salt, and baking soda. 2) In the bowl of a stand mixer fitted with a paddle, beat the butter on medium speed until creamy, 1 minute. Add the granulated and brown sugars and beat on medium speed until light and fluffy, 2 to 3 minutes. Add the vanilla and mix on medium speed until combined. Add the flour mixture and mix on low speed until just combined (the mixture will be crumbly), then add the heavy cream and mix until completely combined and the dough is coming together. Wrap the dough in plastic wrap and chill in the refrigerator until cool but not firm, about 30 minutes. 3) Position an oven rack in the middle of the oven and preheat the oven to 350°F [180°C]. Line three sheet pans with parchment paper. 4) Lightly dust your

100

work surface with cocoa powder. Roll the dough ⅛ in [4 mm] thick. Use a 1 in [2.5 cm] biscuit cutter to cut out rounds. The dough scraps can be rerolled and cut out multiple times. (This dough is very forgiving, so if it cracks as you are rolling it out, you can gently press it back together.) Place the rounds on the prepared sheet pans, fitting about 20 cookies on each pan. 5) Bake the cookies one pan at a time, for 8 to 10 minutes. The cookies will puff up slightly while baking and then fall down when they are baked through. 6) Transfer the pan to a wire rack and let the cookies cool completely (the cookies will crisp up as they cool). Store in an airtight container at room temperature for up to 1 week or in the freezer for up to 1 month.

CHAPTER 8

Extras

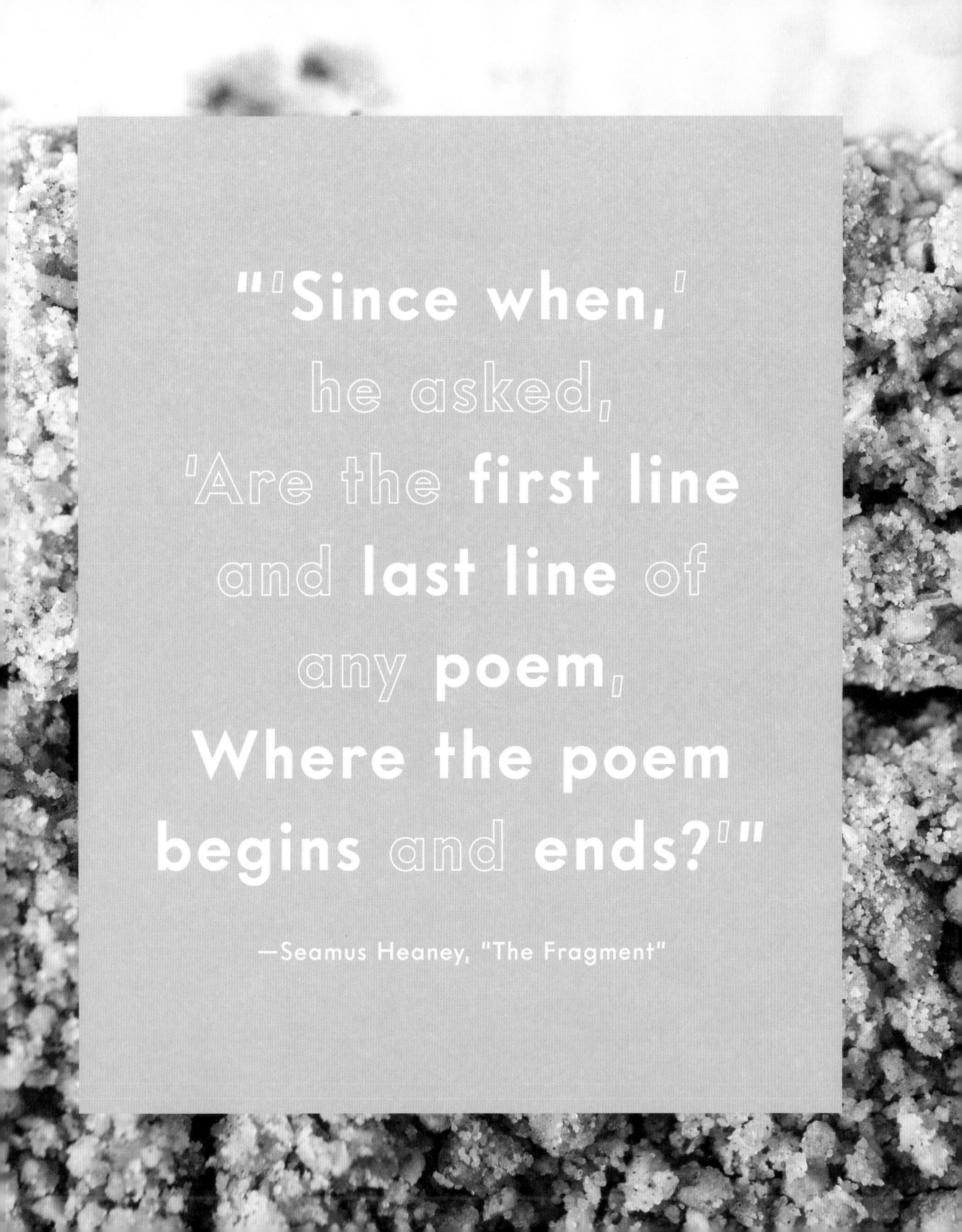

"'Since when,'
he asked,
'Are the **first line**
and **last line** of
any **poem**,
Where the poem
begins and ends?'"

—Seamus Heaney, "The Fragment"

Caramel

This staple is fine store-bought, but so much better homemade. It is a perfect topping to the No-Churn Ice Creams (page 283).

MAKES 1½ CUPS [270 G]

1¼ cups [250 g] granulated sugar

⅓ cup [80 g] water

2 tablespoons corn syrup

½ teaspoon salt

½ cup [120 g] heavy cream

5 tablespoons [70 g] unsalted butter, cut into 5 pieces

1 tablespoon pure vanilla extract

In a large, heavy-bottom saucepan (a deep pan since the caramel will bubble), combine the granulated sugar, water, corn syrup, and salt, stirring very gently to combine while trying to avoid getting any sugar crystals on the side of the pan. Cover the pan, bring to a boil over medium-high heat, and boil until the sugar has melted and the mixture is clear, 3 to 5 minutes. Uncover, then cook until the sugar has turned light golden. Turn the heat down to medium and cook until the sugar has turned deep golden and registers 340°F [170°C] on an instant-read thermometer. Remove immediately from the heat and carefully add the heavy cream. (The cream will foam considerably.) Add the butter, followed by the vanilla, and stir to combine. Set aside to cool. The caramel can be refrigerated for 2 weeks.

VARIATION

• **Salted Caramel:** *When you take the caramel off the heat, add ½ teaspoon of fleur de sel or other flaky salt along with the vanilla.*

Brown Butter

Brown butter adds a nutty flavor to many dishes, but it's not a perfect swap for regular butter in most recipes, as some of the liquid evaporates from the butter as it cooks. You can use any amount of butter for this; the process will be the same.

Unsalted butter

In a light-color, heavy-bottom skillet over medium-low heat, melt the butter. As the butter begins to melt, swirl it around the pan with a rubber spatula. When it starts to bubble, increase the heat to medium and keep stirring until it boils and begins to foam, 3 to 5 minutes. You will start to see brown bits at the bottom of the skillet, and it will begin to smell nutty. Keep stirring, making sure to gently scrape the bottom of the skillet with the spatula as you do so. The butter will quickly change from light brown to dark brown at this point, so keep a close eye on the skillet. Once it is golden brown, remove it from the heat and pour the butter and any flecks on the bottom of the pan into a heatproof bowl. The brown butter can be used immediately or cooled to room temperature and stored in the refrigerator for up to 5 days.

Crème Fraîche

Crème fraîche is similar to sour cream but with a gentler tang and a higher percentage of butterfat. When introduced to high temperatures in a savory tart or sauce, it doesn't break.

MAKES ABOUT 4 CUPS [960 G]

3 cups [720 g] heavy cream

¾ cup [180 g] buttermilk

In a large bowl, whisk together the cream and buttermilk. Cover the top of the bowl with several layers of cheesecloth and place a rubber band or tie a string around the bowl to keep the cheesecloth in place. Let the bowl sit out at room temperature for 24 hours and up to 3 days until it has thickened considerably. (The time it needs depends on the temperature inside your home; cold winter days will cause the mixture to take much longer to thicken than hot summer ones.) When it is thick and ready to use, gently stir the mixture and transfer it to an airtight container. Refrigerate the mixture for up to 1 week.

> **NOTE** Buttermilk contains active cultures ("good" bacteria) that prevent the cream from spoiling and is acidic enough to deter "bad" bacteria from growing.

Whipped Cream

Homemade whipped cream is so delicious and really simple to make. Recently, Zoë François schooled me on my whipped-creaming technique; she insists that low and slow whipping, finished by hand, is the way to go for perfect whipped cream. Of course, she was right. Finishing by hand gives you more control, preventing over-whipping.

MAKES ABOUT 3 CUPS [720 ML]

1½ cups [360 g] heavy cream

2 teaspoons pure vanilla extract

2 tablespoons granulated sugar or confectioners' sugar (see note, page 279)

Pinch of salt (optional; see note, page 279)

1) Ten minutes before whipping the cream, place the bowl and whisk from a stand mixer in the freezer (if it doesn't fit in your freezer, you can refrigerate for 20 minutes instead). **2)** In the chilled bowl of the stand mixer fitted with a chilled whisk, whisk together the heavy cream, granulated sugar, vanilla, and salt (if using) on low speed for 30 to 45 seconds. Increase the speed to medium and beat for 2 to 3 minutes, until the cream is thick and nearly doubled in volume. **3)** Remove the bowl from the mixer and continue whisking by hand (you can use the whisk attachment or a handheld whisk) to your desired consistency. Whipped cream is best used right away, but it can be stored in an airtight container in the refrigerator for up to 2 hours.

NOTE Confectioners' sugar melts faster than granulated, so some bakers prefer using it. I mostly use granulated because I always have it on hand. A pinch of salt isn't needed, but I add it occasionally if the dessert I'm serving is extra sweet.

VARIATIONS

• **Caramel Whipped Cream:** *In the bowl of a stand mixer fitted with a whisk, add 1 cup [240 g] of heavy cream and ½ cup [170 g] of Caramel (page 276), at room temperature. Whisk on low speed for 30 to 45 seconds, until combined. Increase the speed to medium and beat until the cream is smooth, thick, and nearly doubled in volume, 3 to 4 minutes. Add 1 teaspoon of pure vanilla extract and mix on low speed until combined.*

• **Mascarpone Whipped Cream:** *In the bowl of a stand mixer fitted with a whisk, add ¾ cup [180 g] of mascarpone, ⅓ cup [65 g] of granulated sugar, and a pinch of salt. Whisk on low speed until combined. Slowly add 1½ cups [360 g] of heavy cream in a steady stream, mixing until combined. Increase the speed to medium and beat until the cream is smooth, thick, and nearly doubled in volume, 3 to 4 minutes. Add 1 teaspoon of pure vanilla extract and mix on low speed until combined.*

• **White Chocolate:** *In a medium, heavy-bottom saucepan over medium-low heat, warm 1 cup [240 g] of heavy cream until bubbles form at the edges. Place 4 oz [113 g] of white chocolate, chopped, into the bowl of a stand mixer. Pour the warm cream over the chocolate, wait 1 minute, then whisk until smooth. Add 1 teaspoon vanilla and whisk to combine. Cover and refrigerate until chilled, at least 1 hour or up to overnight. Fit a stand mixer with the whisk and beat the mixture on low speed until frothy, then raise the speed to medium and beat until smooth, thick, and nearly doubled in volume, 3 to 4 minutes.*

Pastry Cream

I use pastry cream in my Pavlova (page 233) and as a filling in many confections, but you can put it to so many other uses in your baking life. It can be flavored, folded into whipped cream for a mousse-like texture, or made into German buttercream (crème mousseline) by beating it with room-temperature butter to a smooth texture. Your working ratio is 1 cup [2 sticks or 227 g] of butter to 2 cups [450 g] of pastry cream.

MAKES ABOUT 2 CUPS [450 G]

5 large egg yolks, at room temperature	1 cup [240 g] whole milk
1¼ cups [250 g] granulated sugar	1 cup [240 g] heavy cream
¼ teaspoon salt	1 tablespoon unsalted butter
1 vanilla bean, seeds scraped, pod reserved	2 teaspoons pure vanilla extract
¼ cup [28 g] cornstarch	

1) In the bowl of a stand mixer fitted with a paddle, beat the egg yolks on low speed. With the mixer running on low speed, slowly add the granulated sugar, followed by the salt and vanilla bean seeds, and increase the speed to medium-high (see note, page 280). Beat for about 5 minutes, until the mixture is very thick and pale yellow. Scrape down the sides of the bowl and add the cornstarch, then mix on low speed until combined.

cont'd

2) In a medium, heavy-bottom saucepan over medium-low heat, warm the milk, heavy cream, and vanilla bean pod until just about to simmer. Remove the pan from the heat and pour the mixture into a medium liquid measuring cup with a pourable spout, leaving the pod behind in the pan. 3) With the mixer running on low speed, very slowly add the hot milk mixture. Mix until completely combined. Transfer the mixture back to the saucepan and cook over medium-low heat, stirring constantly with a wooden spoon for 5 to 7 minutes, until the pastry cream becomes very thick and begins to boil. Switch to a whisk and whisk the mixture for 3 to 4 minutes, until the pastry cream thickens and is glossy and smooth. Remove the pan from the heat and strain the pastry cream through a fine-mesh sieve into a medium bowl. Stir in the butter and vanilla. Cover with plastic wrap, making sure the wrap sits directly on top of the cream (this will help keep it from forming a skin). Place in the refrigerator until well chilled. Use right away or keep refrigerated in an air-tight container for 4 to 5 days.

NOTE If the egg yolks are left alone with the sugar, the sugar can burn the yolk, causing it to harden and form little egg bits in whatever you are making. Make sure to continuously whisk the yolks while adding sugar.

Almond Cream

Almond cream, a.k.a. frangipane cream, is used frequently in traditional French baking. There are many ways to make it: with pastry cream, extra egg yolk, almond paste, brandy, or orange essence. Most recipes contain quite a bit of sugar, but since I usually use almond cream in a rich, sugary pastry, I add less. I use almond meal instead of breaking down almonds in the food processor; it saves an extra step and tastes just as good.

In the bowl of a stand mixer fitted with a paddle, beat the butter on medium speed until creamy, about 1 minute. Add the granulated sugar and salt and mix for 1 to 2 minutes, until creamy and combined. Add the almond meal and all-purpose flour and mix until combined, then add the egg and mix again, scraping down the sides as needed, until combined. The mixture may look broken at this point, but that is normal. Add the brandy (if using) and almond extract and stir to combine. The cream will keep in an airtight container in the refrigerator for up to 1 week.

MAKES 1 CUP [300 G]

4 tablespoons [56 g] unsalted butter, at room temperature

¼ cup [50 g] granulated sugar

Pinch of salt

½ cup [50 g] almond meal

3 tablespoons all-purpose flour

1 large egg, at room temperature

1 tablespoon brandy (optional)

⅛ teaspoon almond extract, or more to taste

NOTE You can stir in ⅓ cup [75 g] of pastry cream at the end for a richer version or replace the brandy with ¼ teaspoon of orange essence.

VARIATION
• **Hazelnut Cream:** *Replace ½ cup [50 g] of almond meal with ½ cup [50 g] of hazelnut flour.*

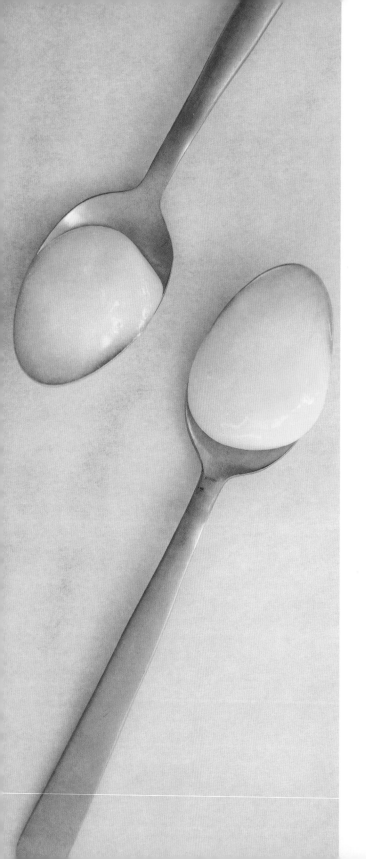

Lemon Curd

Store-bought lemon curd is often too sweet or metallic tasting, so I find that making it at home with fresh lemons is well worth the effort. I leave out the zest for a smooth, not-too-tart curd, but you can add some to ramp up the lemon flavor.

MAKES ABOUT 2 CUPS [640 G]

8 tablespoons [1 stick or 113 g] unsalted butter, at room temperature

1½ cups [250 g] granulated sugar

¼ teaspoon salt

5 large egg yolks, at room temperature

1 large egg, at room temperature

⅓ cup [80 g] fresh lemon juice

1) In the bowl of a stand mixer fitted with a paddle, beat the butter on medium speed until creamy, about 1 minute. Add the granulated sugar and salt and mix on medium speed until combined, 1 minute more. Scrape down the sides of the bowl and add the egg yolks on low speed. Increase the speed to medium and beat for 3 to 4 minutes, until smooth and light. Add the whole egg and mix on low speed until combined, then add the lemon juice and mix on low speed, stopping to scrape down the sides of the bowl as needed. 2) Transfer the mixture to a medium, heavy-bottom saucepan. Cook over medium heat, stirring constantly with a spatula, until the curd becomes very thick, about 10 minutes, or registers 170°F [75°C] on an instant-read thermometer; the mixture should coat a spatula at this point. Strain the mixture through a fine-mesh sieve into a medium bowl, then

cover with plastic wrap, making sure the wrap sits directly on top of the curd (this will help keep it from forming a skin). Place in the refrigerator until well chilled. The curd can be stored in the refrigerator in an airtight container for up to 5 days.

NOTE Add 2 tablespoons of lemon zest to the mixing bowl with the granulated sugar for a lemon curd with a tarter, more acidic flavor.

VARIATIONS

• **Blood Orange Curd:** *Replace the lemon juice with ⅓ cup [80 g] of blood orange juice.*

• **Passion Fruit Curd:** *Replace the lemon juice with ⅓ cup [80 g] of passion fruit purée.*

No-Churn Ice Cream

I had a whole chapter of no-churn ice cream in my first book, *The Vanilla Bean Baking Book*, and I find it a welcome alternative to churning homemade ice cream, as it takes less time and doesn't need an expensive machine.

MAKES ABOUT 4 CUPS [960 G]

One 14 oz [396 g] can sweetened condensed milk

1 tablespoon pure vanilla extract

1 vanilla bean, seeds scraped (optional)

¼ teaspoon salt

2 oz [57 g] cream cheese, at room temperature

2 cups [480 g] heavy cream

1) In a large bowl, whisk together the sweetened condensed milk, vanilla extract, vanilla bean seeds (if using), and salt until completely combined. 2) In the bowl of a stand mixer fitted with a whisk, beat the cream cheese on medium speed until smooth. Turn the mixer to low speed and add the heavy cream in a slow, steady stream, mixing until combined. Increase the speed to medium-high and whisk until stiff peaks form, 3 to 4 minutes. 3) Add half of the whipped cream mixture to the sweetened condensed milk mixture and whisk until completely combined. Using a rubber spatula, gently fold in the remaining whipped cream mixture until no streaks remain. Pour into a 9 by 4 in [23 by 10 cm] Pullman loaf pan (see note, page 284) and freeze until firm, 6 hours, or up to 1 week.

cont'd

NOTE If you don't have a Pullman pan, a regular 9 in [23 cm] loaf pan covered with plastic wrap will work too.

VARIATIONS

• **Coffee No-Churn Ice Cream:** *Add ½ cup [120 g] of room-temperature brewed espresso or strong coffee and ½ teaspoon of ground espresso to the sweetened condensed milk mixture.*

• **Salted Caramel No-Churn Ice Cream:** *Make the no-churn ice cream as directed. Pour half of the ice cream mixture into the Pullman pan, then dollop ½ cup [180 g] of Caramel, salted caramel variation (page 276), over the ice cream. Use the tip of a butter knife to swirl the mixture into the ice cream. Pour the remaining ice cream on top, then dollop with another ½ cup [180 g] of salted caramel. Swirl again with the butter knife. Freeze as directed.*

• **Pumpkin No-Churn Ice Cream:** *Add ¾ cup [168 g] of unsweetened pumpkin purée, ½ teaspoon of ground cinnamon, ¼ teaspoon of ground ginger, ¼ teaspoon of freshly grated nutmeg, and a pinch of cloves to the sweetened condensed milk mixture.*

• **Chocolate No-Churn Ice Cream:** *Melt 8 oz [226 g] of semisweet or bittersweet chocolate. Pour 5 oz [142 g] of the chocolate onto a sheet pan lined with parchment and freeze until firm, 10 to 15 minutes. Add the remaining 3 oz [85 g] of melted chocolate to the sweetened condensed milk mixture. Chop the cold chocolate into bite-size pieces and add it to the finished ice cream mixture before pouring it into the loaf pan.*

• **Peanut Butter No-Churn Ice Cream:** *Add ⅓ cup [72 g] of creamy peanut butter and ½ teaspoon of lemon juice to the sweetened condensed milk mixture. For extra peanut butter flavor, crush 4 to 6 store-bought peanut butter cups and stir them into the mixture.*

Candied Nuts

Nuts are perfect by their lonesome, but adding caramelized sugar and salt elevates them to extraordinary. These are a great textural addition to cakes and confections.

MAKES ABOUT 3 CUPS [380 G]

2 cups [280 g] walnuts, black walnuts, pecans, peanuts, hazelnuts, cashews, almonds, or pepitas, or a combination

½ cup [100 g] granulated sugar

¼ teaspoon salt

1) Line a sheet pan with parchment paper.

2) In a large skillet over medium heat, stir together the nuts, granulated sugar, and salt. Cook until the sugar begins to melt and the nuts begin to toast, stirring constantly. Once the sugar begins to melt, lower the heat to low and cook until the nuts are lightly caramelized. Pour onto the prepared pan and cool completely before chopping. Store in an airtight container at room temperature for up to 1 week.

Streusel

I keep a bag of streusel in my freezer, and it comes in handy quite often. I use it to top the Lemon Streusel Squares (page 188), banana bread, muffins, Bundt cakes, and so on. Baked up on its own, it's a crunchy addition to a bowl of oatmeal, yogurt, or ice cream.

MAKES 4 CUPS [500 G]

1⅓ cups [189 g] all-purpose flour

1 cup [100 g] almond flour

⅔ cup [130 g] granulated sugar

⅔ cup [130 g] brown sugar

1 tablespoon ground cinnamon

¼ teaspoon salt

12 tablespoons [1½ sticks or 170 g] unsalted butter, at room temperature, cut into 12 pieces

In the bowl of a stand mixer fitted with a paddle, combine the all-purpose and almond flours, granulated and brown sugars, cinnamon, and salt on low speed. With the mixer running on low speed, add the butter, one piece at a time, until the mixture comes together but is still quite crumbly. Store the streusel in an airtight container in the refrigerator for up to 1 week, or freeze in a freezer-safe bag for up to 1 month.

Pecan Streusel

Pecans bring extra crunch and toasty nut flavor to anything you sprinkle this streusel over.

MAKES 5 CUPS [740 G]

1½ cups [210 g] toasted pecans, chopped small

1⅓ cups [189 g] all-purpose flour

⅔ cup [130 g] granulated sugar

⅔ cup [130 g] brown sugar

2 teaspoons ground cinnamon

½ teaspoon salt

10 tablespoons [140 g] unsalted butter, melted

In a large bowl, mix together the pecans, flour, granulated and brown sugars, cinnamon, and salt. Pour the melted butter over the top and use a spatula to stir everything together until combined. Store the streusel in an airtight container in the refrigerator for up to 1 week, or freeze in a freezer-safe bag for up to 1 month.

Candied Cacao Nibs

Tara O'Brady's wonderful book, *Seven Spoons*, introduced me to candied cacao nibs years ago. They make a delicious addition to the Brownies 2.0 recipe (page 64), and they're a perfect crunchy-hit-of-chocolatey topping to a scoop of ice cream.

MAKES ABOUT 2½ CUPS [300 G]

2 cups [240 g] cacao nibs

½ cup [100 g] granulated sugar

Pinch of salt

1) Line a sheet pan with parchment paper.

2) In a large skillet over medium heat, stir together the cacao nibs, granulated sugar, and salt. Cook until the sugar begins to melt and the cacao nibs begin to toast, stirring almost constantly. Lower the heat to low and cook until the cacao nibs are lightly caramelized. Pour onto the prepared pan and cool completely before chopping. Store in an airtight container at room temperature for up to 1 week.

Chocolate Magic Shell

Just as its name states, this recipe is magic. When this warm, chocolatey topping hits the cold, creamy ice cream, it hardens almost instantly, creating a crunchy shell that is downright delicious. It will taste fantastic on any of the No-Churn Ice Cream (page 283) variations, but I especially love it on the peanut butter version.

MAKES ABOUT 1¼ CUPS [230 G]

1 cup [170 g] semisweet or bittersweet chocolate chips

¼ cup [60 g] refined coconut oil

Place the chocolate chips and coconut oil in a large liquid measuring cup or other microwave-safe dish. Microwave on high for 30 seconds, then stir. Repeat until the mixture is melted and completely smooth. Let cool slightly, and then pour over ice cream. The magic shell will keep for several months stored at room temperature. If the magic shell hardens, you can gently reheat it in the microwave.

NOTE Extra-virgin coconut oil does not work as well here because it will make the magic shell taste like coconut. Refined coconut oil has a subtler flavor.

MUSIC TO BAKE TO

FEIST
Multitudes

MILES DAVIS
Bye Bye Blackbird

BOYGENIUS
The Record

SORCHA RICHARDSON
Smiling Like an Idiot

BEBEL GILBERTO
Joao

MULATU ASTATKE
Afro-Latin Soul

GRAVEYARD CLUB
Moonflower

ELLA FITZGERALD
Mack the Knife

LIANNE LA HAVAS
Is Your Love Big Enough?

OSCAR PETERSON
Plays Pretty

SUNNY DAY REAL ESTATE
The Rising Tide

JEFF BUCKLEY
Sketches for My Sweetheart the Drunk

Conversions

Commonly Used Ingredients	Oven Temperatures	Weights
1 cup flour = 142 g	300°F = 150°C	½ oz = 14 g
1 cup granulated sugar = 200 g	350°F = 180°C	1 oz = 28 g
1 cup brown sugar = 200 g	375°F = 190°C	1½ oz = 45 g
1 cup confectioners' sugar = 120 g	400°F = 200°C	2 oz = 57 g
1 cup cocoa powder = 100 g	425°F = 220°C	2½ oz = 71 g
1 cup butter (2 sticks) = 227 g	450°F = 230°C	3 oz = 85 g
1 large egg white = 35 g		3½ oz = 99 g
1 cup whole milk = 240 g		4 oz = 113 g
1 cup heavy cream = 240 g		4½ oz = 128 g
1 cup sour cream = 240 g		5 oz = 142 g
1 cup cream cheese = 226 g		8 oz = 226 g
		10 oz = 283 g
		12 oz = 340 g
		16 oz = 455 g

Bibliography

Much of my baking training was hands-on, workplace experience, and many of my ideas, techniques, and recipe evolutions were picked up here and there over the years. It would be impossible to cite everything and everyone, but I must acknowledge (with so much gratitude) Larry and Colleen Wolner and Zoë François for their mentorship, guidance, and encouragement (you can sample the Wolners' amazing baked goods at The Blue Heron Coffeehouse in Winona, Minnesota. And Zoë offers help to all on her beautiful website, zoebakes.com, and her Instagram, @zoebakes).

Over the years, many books have taught me new techniques and guided my baking knowledge. As Lindsey Remolif Shere wrote in her book *Chez Panisse Desserts*, "No cook starts absolutely fresh: there are thousands of contributors to the continuously evolving art of cookery." Here are some who have inspired a starting point or answered a baking question for this book.

Ansel, Dominique. *Everyone Can Bake*. New York: Simon & Schuster, 2020.

Arefi, Yossy. *Snacking Cakes*. Berkeley: Ten Speed Press, 2020.

Barrow, Cathy. *Pie Squared*. New York: Hachette Book Group, 2018.

Braker, Flo. *The Simple Art of Perfect Baking*. San Francisco: Chronicle Books, 1985.

Chang, Joanne. *Pastry Love*. Boston: Houghton Mifflin Harcourt, 2019.

Chesnakova, Polina. *Everyday Cake*. Seattle: Sasquatch Books, 2022.

François, Zoë. *Zoë Bakes Cakes*. Berkeley: Ten Speed Press, 2021.

Greenspan, Dorie. *Baking with Dorie*. Boston: Houghton Mifflin Harcourt, 2021.

Greenstein, George. *A Jewish Baker's Pastry Secrets*. Berkley: Ten Speed Press, 2015.

Heatter, Maida. *Book of Great Desserts*. New York: Knopf, 1965.

Lee, Mandy. *The Art of Escapism Cooking*. New York: Harper Collins Publishers, 2019.

Lin, Irvin. *Marbled, Swirled, and Layered*. New York: Houghton Mifflin Harcourt, 2016.

Lomas, Vallery. *Life Is What You Bake It*. New York: Clarkson Potter, 2021.

O'Brady, Tara. *Seven Spoons*. Berkeley: Ten Speed Press, 2015.

Ottolenghi, Yotam, and Helen Goh. *Sweet*. New York: Ten Speed Press, 2017.

Page, Karen, and Andrew Dorenburg. *The Flavor Bible*. New York: Little, Brown and Company, 2008.

Paredez, Petra "Petee." *Pie for Everyone*. New York: Abrams, 2020.

Prueitt, Elisabeth, and Chad Robertson. *Tartine: A Classic Revisited*. San Francisco: Chronicle, 2019.

Shere, Lindsey Remolif. *Chez Panisse Desserts*. New York: Random House, 1985.

Weller, Melissa. *A Good Bake*. New York: Knopf, 2020.

Wood, Phoebe, and Kirsten Jenkins. *The Pie Project*. London: Hardie Books, 2016.

Resources

BREVILLE
www.breville.com
Kitchen equipment and essentials

COPPERMILL KITCHEN
coppermillkitchen.com
Copper cookware

EMILE HENRY
www.emilehenry.com
Ceramic cookware

KERRYGOLD
www.kerrygoldusa.com
European butter

KING ARTHUR BAKING
www.kingarthurbaking.com
Specialty flours and baking items

MATERIAL
materialkitchen.com
Beautiful and functional kitchen knives and cookware

NORDIC WARE
www.nordicware.com
Baking pans and kitchen necessities

PENZEYS SPICES
www.penzeys.com
Spices

VALRHONA
www.valrhona-chocolate.com
Chocolates and cocoa powder

VERMONT CREAMERY
www.vermontcreamery.com
Butter and other fine dairy products

VOLLRATH
www.vollrathfoodservice.com
Disher scoops that don't break

WILLIAMS SONOMA
www.williams-sonoma.com
Bakeware, baking utensils, and decorating tools

You can also find my favorite kitchen items at my Amazon storefront: amazon.com/shop/sarah_kieffer

Acknowledgments

First, always, thank you to my family: Adam, Winter, and River, for your support and encouragement. Your constant love and help are truly the rocks that this book was built on.

Thank you, Jane Dystel, for all your guidance over the past decade and for always knowing what the next book should be. Thank you also to Miriam Goderich for all your help and expertise.

Thank you, Chronicle Books, and of course Sarah Billingsley. I pinch myself every time I realize I get to write books for my job, and I feel so grateful each day when I head to my kitchen counter to test recipes. Thank you for caring so much about books, and for caring to make a book together. To Lizzie Vaughan, I am so glad to be designing another book with you; you have made these books so beautiful. Thank you to the rest of my Chronicle team: Margo Winton Parodi, Jessica Ling, Tera Killip, Steve Kim, Gabby Vanacore, Keely Thomas-Menter, Alex Galou, Mary Cassells, and Erin Slonaker.

To Amanda Paa, thank you again for all your organization and care. I am so grateful for your friendship and to have you on my team.

To Sara Bartus, another book tested thoroughly by you, and thank goodness! Your honesty and attention helped shape these recipes.

Thank you again to the Blue Heron bakers for baking and testing many of these recipes! I love seeing them and your variations of them in your coffee shop.

To Zoë François, I'm eternally grateful for you. I'm so thankful for your friendship and all your kindness over the years. Everybody loves you.

To all the grandmas and grandpas and aunties and uncles and cousins and dear friends who have stopped by to pick up treats, sent kind words, babysat children, tested recipes, and offered to wash dishes: Thank you. I love you all so much.

And of course, all the lovely *Vanilla Bean Blog* readers. This book wouldn't be here without your support, and I am truly grateful each and every day. Thank you for making my recipes, pan-banging, sending kind notes, buying books, and being so wonderful. Much love.

Index

almonds
    Almond Cream, 281
    Apricot Almond Croissant, 234
    Candied Nuts, 284
    flour, 21
    Picnic Cakes, 227–29
    Raspberry Almond Coffee Cake
    Squares, 174–75
American Buttercream, 245
Apple Cider Pie, 118–19
apricot jam
    Apricot Almond Croissant, 234
    Jam-Filled Doughnut Cake, 50–51

baking powder, 21
baking soda, 21
baking tips, 12–13, 15–17
bananas
    Banana Bread Bars, 45
    Banana Bread Brownies, 72–73
    Banana Bread Cake with Streusel,
    45
    Banana Cream Pie, 132–33
    Brown Butter Banana Blondies,
    74–75
bars
    Banana Bread Bars, 45
    Blueberry Crumble Bars, 178–79
    Brownie Cheesecake Bars, 215–17
    Caramel Rhubarb Shortbread Bars,
    192–93
    Cherry Pie Bars, 182–84
    Chocolate Chip Bars, 97
    Chocolate Meringue Bars, 92–93
    Chocolate Rye Cookie Bars, 90–91
    Creamy Raspberry Bars, 86–87
    Kitchen Sink Crispy Treats, 153
    M&M's Bars, 97
    Mint Chocolate Ice Cream Bars,
    138–39
    Neapolitan Ice Cream Bars,
    148–49

    Oatmeal Fudge Bars, 98–99
    Peanut Butter Chocolate Bars,
    156–57
    Pecan Espresso Bars, 94–95
    Pumpkin Bars, 180–81
    Raisin Rum Bars, 84–85
    S'mores Bars, 159–60
    Strawberry Balsamic Shortcake Ice
    Cream Bars, 145–47
    Sugar Cookie Bars, 82–83
Basil Buttercream, 248
berries. *See also individual berries*
    Mixed Berry Cheesecake Slab Pie,
    121–22
    Pavlova, 233
Birthday Cake, Classic, 52–53
blackberries
    Mixed Berry Cheesecake Slab Pie,
    121–22
blondies
    Bourbon Blondies, 76–77
    Brown Butter Banana Blondies,
    74–75
    Coffee Blondies, 171
    Scotcharoo Blondies, 78–79
    Toasted Sesame Blondies, 81
Blood Orange Curd, 283
blueberries
    Blueberry Buttercream, 243
    Blueberry Crumble Bars, 178–79
    Blueberry Muffin Cake, 42–43
    Flag Cake, 187
    Mixed Berry Cheesecake Slab Pie,
    121–22
bourbon
    Bourbon Blondies, 76–77
    Maple Bourbon Sticky Bun Cake,
    204–6
    Smoky Butterscotch Cream Pie,
    112–13
Brown Butter, 276
    Brown Butter Banana Blondies,
    74–75
brownies
    Banana Bread Brownies, 72–73
    Brownie Cheesecake Bars, 215–17
    Brownies 2.0, 64–65
    Extra-Rich Brownies, 65

    Milk Chocolate Swirl Brownies,
    67–68
    Rocky Road Brownies, 172–73
    White Chocolate, Dark Chocolate
    Brownies, 69–71
brown sugar
    about, 20
    Brown Sugar Buttercream, 243
    Brown Sugar Meringue, 259
butter
    about, 19
    Brown Butter, 276
    Fig Butter, 212, 214
buttercreams
    American Buttercream, 245
    Basil Buttercream, 248
    Bittersweet Chocolate Buttercream,
    254
    Blueberry Buttercream, 243
    Brown Sugar Buttercream, 243
    Cardamom Buttercream, 248
    Coconut Buttercream, 248
    Coffee Buttercream, 248
    Cream Cheese Buttercream, 250
    Ermine Buttercream, 246–48
    Espresso Buttercream, 245
    Fudge Buttercream, 256
    Green Tea Buttercream, 248
    Irish Cream Buttercream, 249
    Lavender Buttercream, 248
    Malt Buttercream, 248
    Peanut Butter Buttercream, 253
    Raspberry American Buttercream,
    245
    Raspberry Swiss Meringue
    Buttercream, 243
    Rosemary Buttercream, 248
    Strawberry Buttercream, 243
    Swiss Meringue Buttercream,
    242–43
    Ultra Buttercream, 249
butterscotch
    Kitchen Sink Crispy Treats, 153
    Scotcharoo Blondies, 78–79
    Smoky Butterscotch Cream Pie,
    112–13

cacao nibs
about, 22
Cacao Nib Meringue, 259
Candied Cacao Nibs, 288
Chocolate Cheesecake, 154–55
Chocolate Meringue Bars, 92–93
Kitchen Sink Crispy Treats, 153
cakes
Banana Bread Bars, 45
Banana Bread Cake with Streusel,
45
Blueberry Muffin Cake, 42–43
Chocolate Cheesecake, 154–55
Chocolate Chip Buttermilk Cake,
218–20
Chocolate Éclair Cake, 161–63
Chocolate Red Wine Cake, 56–57
Classic Birthday Cake, 52–53
Classic Crumb Cake, 34–35
Coconut Chocolate Chip Cake,
54–55
Confetti Cake with Berry
Buttercream, 32–33
Cranberry Caramel Upside-Down
Cake, 40–41
Double Chocolate Cake, 58–59
Flag Cake, 187
Gluten-Free Cake, 236–37
Hazelnut Frangipane Cake, 207–9
Honey Sesame Cake, 49
Jam-Filled Doughnut Cake, 50–51
Lemon Cake Squares, 88–89
Maple Bourbon Sticky Bun Cake,
204–6
Maple Orange Carrot Cake,
46–47
Minnesota Sheet Cake, 196–97
My Perfect Afternoon Snack Cake,
30–31
Orange-Cinnamon Swirl Cake,
202–3
Peanut Butter and Jelly Cake,
194–95
Picnic Cakes, 227–29
Pumpkin Caramel Ice Cream Cake,
143–44
Raspberry Almond Coffee Cake
Squares, 174–75
Raspberry Poppy Seed Cake,
38–39
Red Velvet Ice Cream Cake,
140–41
Show-Stopper Carrot Cake, 47

Straight-Up Yellow Snacking Cake,
37
Strawberry Shortcake Cake,
185–87
Sunken Chocolate Cake, 210–11
Tiramisu Cake, 221–23
White Chocolate Cheesecake,
224–26
canola oil, 20
Caramel, 276
Caramel Rhubarb Shortbread Bars,
192–93
Caramel Whipped Cream, 279
Cranberry Caramel Upside-Down
Cake, 40–41
Pumpkin Caramel Ice Cream Cake,
143–44
Salted Caramel No-Churn Ice
Cream, 284
Cardamom Buttercream, 248
carrots
Maple Orange Carrot Cake,
46–47
Show-Stopper Carrot Cake, 47
cashews
Candied Nuts, 284
Cheater Croissant Dough, 264–65
cheese. *See* cream cheese;
mascarpone
cheesecake
Brownie Cheesecake Bars, 215–17
Chocolate Cheesecake, 154–55
Mixed Berry Cheesecake Slab Pie,
121–22
Raspberry Mascarpone
Cheesecake Tart, 176–77
White Chocolate Cheesecake,
224–26
Cherry Pie Bars, 182–84
chocolate. *See also* cacao nibs; white
chocolate
Banana Bread Brownies, 72–73
Bittersweet Chocolate Buttercream,
254
Bourbon Blondies, 76–77
Brownie Cheesecake Bars, 215–17
Brownies 2.0, 64–65
Chocolate Cheesecake, 154–55
Chocolate Chip Bars, 97
Chocolate Chip Buttermilk Cake,
218–20
Chocolate Éclair Cake, 161–63
Chocolate Glaze, 159–60
Chocolate Irish Cream Mousse Pie,
110–11
Chocolate Magic Shell, 288
Chocolate Meringue Bars, 92–93

Chocolate Mousse, 110–11
Chocolate No-Churn Ice Cream,
284
Chocolate Peanut Butter Pie, 107–9
Chocolate Red Wine Cake, 56–57
Chocolate Rye Cookie Bars, 90–91
Chocolate Wafer Cookies, 22,
270–71
Classic Birthday Cake, 52–53
Coconut Chocolate Chip Cake,
54–55
Coffee Blondies, 171
Double Chocolate Cake, 58–59
Extra-Rich Brownies, 65
Fudge Buttercream, 256
Ganache, 257
Half-Sheet Pan Ganache, 257
Irish Cream Ganache, 110–11
Kitchen Sink Crispy Treats, 153
melting, 21
Milk Chocolate Swirl Brownies,
67–68
Millionaire Pie, 105–6
Minnesota Sheet Cake, 196–97
Mint Chocolate Ice Cream Bars,
138–39
Neapolitan Ice Cream Bars,
148–49
Oatmeal Fudge Bars, 98–99
Passion Fruit S'mores Pie, 123–24
Peanut Butter Chocolate Bars,
156–57
Pecan Espresso Bars, 94–95
Rocky Road Brownies, 172–73
Scotcharoo Blondies, 78–79
S'mores Bars, 159–60
Sunken Chocolate Cake, 210–11
tempering, 16
Tiramisu Cake, 221–23
types of, 21–22
White Chocolate, Dark Chocolate
Brownies, 69–71
White Chocolate Raspberry
Squares, 164–65
coconut
Coconut Buttercream, 248
Coconut Chocolate Chip Cake,
54–55
coffee
Chocolate Meringue Bars, 92–93
Coffee Blondies, 171
Coffee Buttercream, 248
Coffee No-Churn Ice Cream, 284
Double Chocolate Cake, 58–59
Espresso Buttercream, 245
Minnesota Sheet Cake, 196–97
Pecan Espresso Bars, 94–95

Sunken Chocolate Cake, 210–11
Tiramisu Cake, 221–23
Confetti Cake with Berry Buttercream, 32–33
Cookies, Chocolate Wafer, 22, 270–71
cooking oils, 20
corn flakes
Peanut Butter Chocolate Bars, 156–57
Cranberry Caramel Upside-Down Cake, 40–41
cream, heavy, 19
cream cheese
about, 19
Brown Butter Banana Blondies, 74–75
Brownie Cheesecake Bars, 215–17
Chocolate Cheesecake, 154–55
Cream Cheese Buttercream, 250
Giant Pop Tart, 230–31
Maple Cream Cheese Icing, 46–47
Mint Chocolate Ice Cream Bars, 138–39
Mixed Berry Cheesecake Slab Pie, 121–22
Pumpkin Bars, 180–81
Raspberry Almond Coffee Cake Squares, 174–75
Raspberry Mascarpone Cheesecake Tart, 176–77
Red Velvet Ice Cream Cake, 140–41
Rhubarb and Cream Hand Pies, 129–31
S'mores Bars, 159–60
Strawberry Balsamic Shortcake Ice Cream Bars, 145–47
Strawberry Shortcake Cake, 185–87
White Chocolate Cheesecake, 224–26
crème fraîche
about, 19
Crème Fraîche Dough, 263
making, 278
croissants
Apricot Almond Croissant, 234
Cheater Croissant Dough, 264–65
Crumb Cake, Classic, 34–35

D

Double Chocolate Cake, 58–59
Doughnut Cake, Jam-Filled, 50–51

E

eggs
about, 19
wash, 16
equipment, 24–25
Ermine Buttercream, 246–48
espresso. *See coffee*

F

figs
Fig Butter, 212, 214
Fig Scones, 212–14
Flag Cake, 187
flours
measuring, 15
protein levels of, 19
types of, 20–21
fruits. *See also individual fruits*
freeze-dried, 16
fudge
Fudge Buttercream, 256
Oatmeal Fudge Bars, 98–99

G

Ganache, 257
Half-Sheet Pan Ganache, 257
Irish Cream Ganache, 110–11
glazes
Chocolate Glaze, 159–60
Lemon Glaze, 88–89
Raspberry Glaze, 38–39
Gluten-Free Cake, 236–37
graham crackers
Banana Cream Pie, 132–33
Chocolate Éclair Cake, 161–63
Passion Fruit S'mores Pie, 123–24
Peanut Butter Chocolate Bars, 156–57
Pumpkin Caramel Ice Cream Cake, 143–44
Raspberry Mascarpone Cheesecake Tart, 176–77
Roasted Strawberry Cream Pie, 125–26
S'mores Bars, 159–60
White Chocolate Cheesecake, 224–26
Green Tea Buttercream, 248

H

hazelnuts
Candied Nuts, 284
flour, 21
Hazelnut Cream, 281
Hazelnut Frangipane Cake, 207–9
Honey Sesame Cake, 49
humidity, role of, 17

I

ice cream
Chocolate No-Churn Ice Cream, 284
Coffee No-Churn Ice Cream, 284
Mint Chocolate Ice Cream Bars, 138–39
Neapolitan Ice Cream Bars, 148–49
No-Churn Ice Cream, 283–84
Peanut Butter No-Churn Ice Cream, 284
Pumpkin Caramel Ice Cream Cake, 143–44
Pumpkin No-Churn Ice Cream, 284
Red Velvet Ice Cream Cake, 140–41
Salted Caramel No-Churn Ice Cream, 284
Strawberry Balsamic Shortcake Ice Cream Bars, 145–47
Icing, Maple Cream Cheese, 46–47
Irish cream
Chocolate Irish Cream Mousse Pie, 110–11
Irish Cream Buttercream, 249
Irish Cream Ganache, 110–11

J

jam. *See also apricot jam*
Giant Pop Tart, 230–31
Jam-Filled Doughnut Cake, 50–51
Rhubarb Jam, 129, 131

K

Kahlúa
Espresso Buttercream, 245
Pecan Espresso Bars, 94–95
Tiramisu Cake, 221–23
Kitchen Sink Crispy Treats, 153

L

Lavender Buttercream, 248
lemons
  Lemon Cake Squares, 88–89
  Lemon Curd, 282–83
  Lemon Glaze, 88–89
  Lemon Meringue Pie, 116–17
  Lemon Streusel Squares, 188
  Lemon White Chocolate Pie, 114
  Pavlova, 233

M

Magic Shell, Chocolate, 288
Malt Buttercream, 248
M&M's Bars, 97
maple syrup
  Maple Bourbon Sticky Bun Cake, 204–6
  Maple Cream Cheese Icing, 46–47
  Maple Orange Carrot Cake, 46–47
marshmallows
  Kitchen Sink Crispy Treats, 153
  Rocky Road Brownies, 172–73
  S'mores Bars, 159–60
mascarpone
  Mascarpone Whipped Cream, 279
  Raspberry Mascarpone Cheesecake Tart, 176–77
  Rhubarb and Cream Hand Pies, 129–31
  Tiramisu Cake, 221–23
measuring, 15, 24
Meringue, 258–59
  Baked Meringues, 259
  Brown Sugar Meringue, 259
  Cacao Nib Meringue, 259
  Chocolate Meringue Bars, 92–93
  Lemon Meringue Pie, 116–17
  Pavlova, 233
  Swiss Meringue Buttercream, 242–43
milk, 19
Millionaire Pie, 105–6
Minnesota Sheet Cake, 196–97
Mint Chocolate Ice Cream Bars, 138–39
Mousse Pie, Chocolate Irish Cream, 110–11
Muffin Cake, Blueberry, 42–43
music, 293

N

Neapolitan Ice Cream Bars, 148–49
No-Churn Ice Cream, 283–84
nuts. *See also individual nuts*
  Candied Nuts, 284
  toasting, 21

O

oats
  Blueberry Crumble Bars, 178–79
  Chocolate Rye Cookie Bars, 90–91
  Creamy Raspberry Bars, 86–87
  Oatmeal Fudge Bars, 98–99
  Raisin Rum Bars, 84–85
olive oil, 20
oranges
  Blood Orange Curd, 283
  Maple Orange Carrot Cake, 46–47
  Orange-Cinnamon Swirl Cake, 202–3
ovens, 16–17

P

pans
  lining, with parchment paper, 16
  rotating, during baking, 17
  types of, 24, 25
passion fruit
  Passion Fruit Curd, 283
  Passion Fruit Slice, 151
  Passion Fruit S'mores Pie, 123–24
Pastry Cream, 279–80
Pat-in-the-Pan Pie Dough, 262
Pavlova, 233
peanuts and peanut butter
  Candied Nuts, 284
  Chocolate Peanut Butter Pie, 107–9
  Giant Pop Tart, 230–31
  Kitchen Sink Crispy Treats, 153
  Peanut Butter and Jelly Cake, 194–95
  Peanut Butter Buttercream, 253
  Peanut Butter Chocolate Bars, 156–57
  Peanut Butter No-Churn Ice Cream, 284
  Rocky Road Brownies, 172–73
  Scotcharoo Blondies, 78–79

pecans
  Candied Nuts, 284
  Chocolate Rye Cookie Bars, 90–91
  Coffee Blondies, 171
  Maple Bourbon Sticky Bun Cake, 204–6
  Minnesota Sheet Cake, 196–97
  Pecan Dough, 262
  Pecan Espresso Bars, 94–95
  Pecan Streusel, 287
  Smoky Butterscotch Cream Pie, 112–13
pepitas
  Candied Nuts, 284
Picnic Cakes, 227–29
Pie Dough, 261
  Crème Fraîche Dough, 263
  Pat-in-the-Pan Pie Dough, 262
  Pecan Dough, 262
pies. *See also* Pie Dough
  Apple Cider Pie, 118–19
  Banana Cream Pie, 132–33
  Cherry Pie Bars, 182–84
  Chocolate Irish Cream Mousse Pie, 110–11
  Chocolate Peanut Butter Pie, 107–9
  Lemon Meringue Pie, 116–17
  Lemon White Chocolate Pie, 114
  Millionaire Pie, 105–6
  Mixed Berry Cheesecake Slab Pie, 121–22
  Passion Fruit S'mores Pie, 123–24
  Pumpkin Streusel Pie, 127–28
  Rhubarb and Cream Hand Pies, 129–31
  Roasted Strawberry Cream Pie, 125–26
  Smoky Butterscotch Cream Pie, 112–13
poppy seeds
  Chocolate Rye Cookie Bars, 90–91
  Lemon Meringue Pie, 116–17
  Picnic Cakes, 227–29
  Raspberry Poppy Seed Cake, 38–39
Pop Tart, Giant, 230–31
potato chips
  Kitchen Sink Crispy Treats, 153
Pretzel Shortbread Fingers, 190–91
puff pastry
  Giant Pop Tart, 230–31
  Rhubarb and Cream Hand Pies, 129–31
  Rough Puff Pastry, 268–69

100 Afternoon Sweets

pumpkin
 Pumpkin Bars, 180–81
 Pumpkin Caramel Ice Cream Cake, 143–44
 Pumpkin No-Churn Ice Cream, 284
 Pumpkin Streusel Pie, 127–28

R

Raisin Rum Bars, 84–85
raspberries
 Creamy Raspberry Bars, 86–87
 Jam-Filled Doughnut Cake, 50–51
 Mixed Berry Cheesecake Slab Pie, 121–22
 Peanut Butter and Jelly Cake, 194–95
 Raspberry Almond Coffee Cake Squares, 174–75
 Raspberry American Buttercream, 245
 Raspberry Glaze, 38–39
 Raspberry Mascarpone Cheesecake Tart, 176–77
 Raspberry Poppy Seed Cake, 38–39
 Raspberry Swiss Meringue Buttercream, 243
 White Chocolate Raspberry Squares, 164–65
Red Velvet Ice Cream Cake, 140–41
rhubarb
 Caramel Rhubarb Shortbread Bars, 192–93
 Rhubarb and Cream Hand Pies, 129–31
 Rhubarb Jam, 129, 131
Rice Krispies cereal
 Kitchen Sink Crispy Treats, 153
 Scotcharoo Blondies, 78–79
Rocky Road Brownies, 172–73
Rosemary Buttercream, 248
rum
 Raisin Rum Bars, 84–85
 Smoky Butterscotch Cream Pie, 112–13
Rye Cookie Bars, Chocolate, 90–91

S

salt, 15, 20
saltine crackers
 Apple Cider Pie, 118–19
Scones, Fig, 212–14
Scotcharoo Blondies, 78–79

sesame oil, toasted
 about, 20
 Honey Sesame Cake, 49
 Toasted Sesame Blondies, 81
sesame seeds
 Chocolate Rye Cookie Bars, 90–91
 Toasted Sesame Blondies, 81
shortbread
 Caramel Rhubarb Shortbread Bars, 192–93
 Millionaire Pie, 105–6
 Pretzel Shortbread Fingers, 190–91
Show-Stopper Carrot Cake, 47
s'mores
 Passion Fruit S'mores Pie, 123–24
 S'mores Bars, 159–60
spices, 20
Sticky Bun Cake, Maple Bourbon, 204–6
strawberries
 Flag Cake, 187
 Neapolitan Ice Cream Bars, 148–49
 Roasted Strawberry Cream Pie, 125–26
 Strawberry Balsamic Shortcake Ice Cream Bars, 145–47
 Strawberry Buttercream, 243
 Strawberry Shortcake Cake, 185–87
Streusel, 287
 Pecan Streusel, 287
sugar. *See also* **brown sugar**
 Sugar Cookie Bars, 82–83
 Sugar Cookie Bars with Frosting, 83
 types of, 20
Sunken Chocolate Cake, 210–11
Swiss Meringue Buttercream, 242–43

T

Tart, Raspberry Mascarpone Cheesecake, 176–77
Tea Buttercream, Green, 248
temperature, role of, 17
Tiramisu Cake, 221–23

U

Ultra Buttercream, 249

V

vanilla, 22

W

walnuts
 Candied Nuts, 284
 Minnesota Sheet Cake, 196–97
Whipped Cream, 278–79
 Caramel Whipped Cream, 279
 Mascarpone Whipped Cream, 279
white chocolate
 about, 22
 Lemon White Chocolate Pie, 114
 White Chocolate Cheesecake, 224–26
 White Chocolate, Dark Chocolate Brownies, 69–71
 White Chocolate Raspberry Squares, 164–65
Wine Cake, Chocolate Red, 56–57

Y

Yellow Snacking Cake, Straight-Up, 37

SEE ALSO

100 COOKIES

100 MORNING TREATS

BAKING FOR THE HOLIDAYS